The LOVE@WORK Method™

Practices and Tools for Stepping Into Your Life of Inspired Purpose

Marina,
Your heart and voice are such a gift. Much love,
Olivia

Olivia Parr-Rud, MS

Quantum Love Press

This book is a work of non-fiction.

For information contact www.oliviapr.com

ISBN: 978-1-7324352-1-6

First Edition: April 2019

"Olivia sees beyond the status quo/current reality into a new vibratory level where the unique gift of each individual is required for the symphony of life to resonate at its fullest magnificence." - Connie Baxter Marlow and Andrew Cameron Bailey, The Trust Frequency

It's a powerful, but easy to use, resource that I will use over and over again for clarity" - Kathy Mason, Author and President, Mason Works

"Olivia brilliantly leads readers on a captivating journey inside 'companies rooted in trust, caring and authenticity'". - Marlene Elizabeth, MONEYWINGS™

"It is not often that we meet an author who is on the pulse of what is needed. Olivia Parr-Rud, has written a book that is timely and will help many people." - Nancy Mills, The Spirited Woman

"What's clear to my mind is that the weaving and braiding necessary for our own developmental journey is only enhanced through the application of the 4 steps into our own unique perspective." - Mike Jay, Developmentalist

"Step by step she leads you into a journey of self-discovery and empowerment." - Julie Ann, Author and Spiritual Coach

To all the souls yearning to make a positive difference in the world.

ACKNOWLEDGEMENTS

This book, as the companion book to LOVE@WORK, *The Essential Guide to a Life of Inspired Purpose*, has been incubating for many years. I have had a few amazing coaches and editors along the way. Thank you, Stevie Ray McHugh, for helping to steer my thinking and for your creative genius. You were instrumental in helping me flesh out the LOVE@WORK Method. Thank you, Michelle Depres, for your wisdom, guidance, and encouragement. It was in your guided visualization that the cover image emerged as well as many ideas for the content of my book. Thank you, Michelle Williams, for helping me find my voice and your masterful editing. Thank you, John Castagnini, for your guidance and encouragement to create he LOVE@WORK Method™ and think about how to take it into the world. Thank you, Carl Gaertner, for your loving feedback and suggestions. Thank you, Kathy Mason, for your amazing spiritual guidance and helping me to fine tune my message. I look forward to creating more with you. Finally, thank you, Rebecca Hall Gruyter, for your huge heart and pure spirit. Thank you for your encouragement to bring out my voice. Thank you for your beautiful foreword, and thank you for bringing the book to life with your amazing book creation and launch team.

I'd like to thank the visionaries that have inspired me. Thank you, Judi Neal, for your leadership in bringing spirituality into business. Thank you, Chris Lazlo, for your genius in leveraging ground-breaking science to create agile holistic organizational models.

Thank you, Riane Eisler, for your lifelong dedication to balancing our divine masculine and divine feminine as well as your work with bringing human values into business through your Center for Partnership Studies. And thank you, Andrew Cameron Bailey and Connie Baxter Marlow, for your brilliance, generous spirits, and huge hearts as you share The Trust Frequency with the world.

I'd also like to thank my family. First, thanks to my sisters, Marjie Gargiulo and Beth White, and sister-in-law, Jill Parr, for your encouragement. Thank you to my kids, Brandon, Adam, and Vanessa Rud, and my daughter-in-law, Allison Rud. You continue to inspire me to be my best.

Finally, I'd like to thank my spiritual tribe who helped me in so many ways. First and foremost, thank you to Joe Diamo. Your generous spirit, unconditional love, and tireless encouragement and guidance towards a deeper spiritual connection were instrumental in helping me to bring this book forward. Thank you, Marilyn Reis, for your thoughtful feedback and amazing editing prowess. I especially appreciate your subtle suggestions for helping me cognize the deeper meaning and clarify my message. Thank you, Caroline 'Patsy' Bell for your dear friendship and being such an awesome coaching partner. Thank you, Janet Straightarrow, for your insights, wisdom, and guidance on my deep healing journey. Thank you, Julie Roberts for your dear friendship and wisdom, and for creating and teaching CLEAR®. Thank you, Antanas Vainius, for your friendship, inspiration, and support. And thank you to my tribe of friends and healers: Mary Hostetter, Glennis Walter Smith, Priya Beate, Adelyn Jones, Lora Terres, Logan Kline, and Dylan Clements, and. You all kept me aligned, feeling good, laughing, and feeling loved and valued. You are all in my hearts forever.

THE BIG "WHY?"

Can you imagine a world in which everyone lives in peace and harmony? Where joy and bliss permeate your everyday experience? Can you let yourself feel that – even for a few seconds? Feels good, doesn't it?

But, if you are like me, your mind steps in and says, "Are you crazy? That's not possible. Look around. The world is full of chaos and division. And it's getting worse!"

While all of this is true, there is something deeper happening. And it's very good.

As we imagine a world of peace and harmony, we need to know not only that it is possible, but that it is not far away. Our ability to imagine it is an important step in the process.

Quantum physics states that we are all energy. We are vibrational beings. Our thoughts matter. So, spending time imagining this world of peace and harmony not only feels good. It is an essential part of bringing this new world into form.

All the great wisdom teachings say that our consciousness is evolving. Many of us feel a growing desire for meaning and purpose. This is natural, and this is good. But how do we get there?

Think of the poor caterpillar as it feels its body starting to harden. It's all part of a natural process, as its body becomes a chrysalis. However, from the caterpillar's perspective, it feels as though it is dying.

Physically, the chrysalis is little more than a toxic soup. Yet, on an energetic level, something very magical is happening. Within this toxic soup there are imaginal cells that eventually evolve into the most beautiful butterfly.

As humans, we are in our chrysalis stage. We are surrounded by this toxic soup. We must keep imagining the world we want to create.

So how can we help?

To create this new world, we must all show up to our fullest extent. This new world we are imagining needs every one of us to step into the greatest version of ourselves. We are all born with unique gifts, which must be revealed, nurtured, and shared.

You are beautiful, perfect, and necessary. You are here for a reason. You have a unique part to play in this new world. There is no one else exactly like you. You are one of a kind. You matter.

So what is stopping you? What is stopping all of us?

Many of us were raised in a culture that profited from telling us that we are not enough. On top of this, we must remember the fact that many of us have experienced so much loss and emotional trauma that we have lost touch with our essence. We doubt our greatness. We look to others for validation. We seek drugs and alcohol to numb our pain. This is not our natural state. This is a symptom of our disconnection from our essence and our natural expression – the true source of our joy.

To summon the courage and strength to truly show up and step into our greatness, we must learn to deeply love ourselves. For many of us, this is a lifelong journey. By committing to this journey, committing to loving ourselves, finding our gifts, and sharing them with the world, we become the greatest version of ourselves. This is something the world needs from us to evolve into the greatest version of herself: the world of peace and joy that we imagine is possible.

HOW TO USE THIS BOOK

My hope is that you found this book because you yearn for more meaning in your life. Perhaps you have a sense that you are here for something greater than you can currently see in your future. You may have a strong desire to make a positive difference in the world. If you resonate with these statements, then this book is for you.

This book is a companion book to LOVE@WORK, *The Essential Guide to a Life of Inspired Purpose*. Each of the steps in this book is designed to take you deeper into the steps of the LOVE@WORK Method™, which support you on the journey to your greatness. I invite you to think of it as your guidebook. Read a little each day. Engage in the exercises. You may digest the content very quickly, but completing the journey may take a lifetime.

Each chapter focuses on a step in the LOVE@WORK Method™. Through collective wisdom, stories, and practices, each chapter is designed to inspire your inner knowing and invite you to take another step on your journey.

As you work through the steps, take time to reflect, write, and share with others. Keep a journal of your experiences and insights. If you feel you need more support, please feel free to contact me through my website oliviapr.com.

FOREWORD

When I first met Olivia, I was impressed by her authenticity, her warmth, and her loving and positive approach to life. As I have gotten to know Olivia on deeper levels, I discovered those first impressions have proven to be true. I can add to the list a brilliant mind, with a unique way of looking at data, patterns, people, and organizations. I believe she can see patterns and trends before the average heart and mind can, and she is able to bring that insight and information forward in a way that is compelling, powerful, and always supportive of positive growth.

She has a commitment to helping all of us imagine the world we want to create, and fully show up in it as the best version of ourselves by stepping into our inspired purpose. I love how in this book she is taking us deeper into her LOVE@WORK Method™, a system with powerful interactive exercises to support us in living a life of inspired purpose. She starts with looking at self-love, providing a powerful assessment and exercise to help you gain clarity on where you currently are and where you may want to bring in additional love for yourself. What a beautiful gift. When we have clarity on where we are and what may be holding love back, we can get support on how to move forward. I believe all of us have room to bring in more love for ourselves and others, and I appreciate Olivia providing such a powerful and loving method to help us step forward, starting with extending more love, grace, and support to ourselves.

Through her powerful book she helps us walk through her four signature steps to help us love all of ourselves, own our superpowers, visualize our inspired purpose, and engage fully with our tribe so that we can live a life of inspired purpose. Olivia has created a transformational system that helps you go deep in a powerful and safe way, so that you can move forward and bring more love into your life, your circle of influence, your businesses, and the world. I know this book will inspire you to take the action necessary to become who you truly want to be and share the powerful gift of who you are with the world!

As an Empowerment Leader, Publisher, Author, Network Owner, Business Coach, Speaker and Publisher, my team and I are in the business of uplifting people around the world, one heart and life at a time. This is exactly what Olivia is doing with her powerful book. We celebrate her bringing her light, knowledge, wisdom, experience, and inspiration to all of us.

I celebrate you leaning in and saying yes to this book, as I know it will bring powerful transformation into your life and your business. I know you will be equipped, encouraged, uplifted, and empowered to embrace and celebrate your journey of stepping more fully into your inspired purpose.

Rebecca Hall Gruyter, Empowerment Leader & Influencer
Committed to helping you make a positive difference around the world...one heart and life at a time!

CEO of RHG Media Productions, RHG TV Network, and Your Purpose Driven Practice.

www.YourPurposeDrivenPractice.com
www.RHGTVNetwork.com
Rebecca@YourPurposeDrivenPractice.com
(925) 787-1572

TABLE OF CONTENTS

INTRODUCTION

The LOVE@WORK Method™ consists of four steps. As you work through the steps, you will be empowered to discover and align with your inspired purpose in your career and in your life. Along the way, you will discover your true self, unveil and release the barriers that get in your way, and learn to show up for yourself and others. The LOVE@WORK Method™ offers techniques and practices to allow you to heal, align with your inspired purpose, and share gifts in the world every day.

Along the way, you will find that by deeply loving yourself and opening your heart, you will tap into your own innate wisdom. This connection to your deepest self will empower you to enjoy unbridled creativity, deeply meaningful relationships, and an abundance of joy at work and at play.

"You are not a drop in the ocean. You are the entire ocean in a drop." - Rumi

A foundational principle of the LOVE@WORK Method™ is that we live in an interconnected, co-creative universe. Therefore, our paths and destinies are integrally connected with everyone and everything on the planet. **Whatever we want to manifest, create, attract, and experience must be desired for the greater good. I**

believe that as we seek to live an inspired life, we increase the chance that everyone on the planet will thrive.

The four steps of the LOVE@WORK Method™ follow a logical sequence. However, it may not be a direct path. Think of it more like a spiral. You will consistently progress to a higher level. But as you move through steps two through four, issues may arise that gently (or not so gently) nudge you back to an earlier step for more self-love, self-ownership, or clarity of purpose. Any time you move ahead to a new step and feel stuck or blocked, the LOVE@ WORK Method™ will guide you back to the appropriate step with a couple of simple questions. Know that if you find yourself going back through each step, you are still progressing.

Step 1: Love All of Yourself

Many of us find it easy to love others but struggle to really love every part of ourselves. And yet if we seek to live an inspired life, we must practice deep self-love and compassion. As we strive to love ourselves, we may experience resistance caused by unconscious patterns, limiting beliefs, and past traumas. This step guides you through practices and techniques for getting to a place of deep self-love. NOTE: Because self-love is foundational to all healthy actions, reactions, and interactions, this step is the foundation of the LOVE@WORK Method™.

Step 2: Own Your Superpower

Many of us yearn to step into our power and express our unique gifts. Once you catch a glimpse of your potential, there is no going back. You can no longer hide your light. **Discovering and owning your superpowers is the next step in creating the career of your dreams and the life you were meant to live.** This step offers tools and practices that serve to unveil your unique gifts and innate wisdom that the world needs you to share.

Step 3: Visualize Your Inspired Purpose

As we gain more insight into our inspired purpose, we can start to imagine, visualize, and gain clarity around who we want to become or how we want to participate in the world. This step guides you to visualize your inspired purpose based on your superpower or superpowers. You create an inspired plan that clarifies how you want to be in the world and builds action steps to move into the world with your inspired purpose.

Step 4: Engage With Your Tribe

Historically, those of us who sought to live an inspired life would spend our lives in a monastery or on a secluded mountaintop. It takes a lot of courage and will power to survive in this world, let alone feel inspired. But as we know, **the world needs us to show up completely and share our gifts. We need to shine our light everywhere we go. This includes the workplace. This step offers strategies for finding ways to open your heart, allow yourself to**

be vulnerable, and enjoy deep connections with your coworkers, your friends, and even yourself. You will learn techniques for finding your inner calm in stressful environments. You will even learn strategies and tools for moving through your fear so you can shine your light, share your authentic self, step into your Inspired Purpose, and engage with your tribe in service to the greater good.

STEP 1: LOVE ALL OF YOURSELF

"The foundation of all joy, vulnerability, resilience, and success is self-love." – Olivia Parr-Rud

What does it mean to love all of yourself? Don't we all have things we don't like about ourselves? Don't we all have things we want to hide?

Yes, we will always find things about ourselves that we wish were better. When I think of who we are – I focus on our essence or spirit. That part of us always deserves of our love.

What is Self-Love?

I feel that self-love is foundational to living an inspired life. Self-love is the core energetic state from which our inspiration flows. This flow allows us to truly show up, share our innate gifts, and make a positive difference in the world.

There many things which self-love is not. I'm sure you have heard someone say, "He loves himself a bit too much!" I'm sure you have experienced that person who always wants to be the center of attention – the narcissist. The sad truth is this person is the one who needs more self-love. A person with a healthy level of self-love is comfortable with attention on oneself while also ensuring that there is a balance by directing attention to or showing appreciation for others.

If you simply practice putting your attention on others, your life will improve. Everyone wants to be seen, heard, and valued. By giving someone that gift, you will often be reciprocated with appreciation and love. All of this seems so simple. But how do we become capable of this?

As we begin **Step 1: Love All of Yourself**, think of it as a lifelong process, and know that it gets easier over time.

Depending on our personal history, our capacity for loving all of ourselves may vary. Those of us that had (or still have) loving supportive parents, lived in safe neighborhoods, and had lots of positive messages as children might have a head start.

On the other hand, those of us who were neglected, abused, abandoned, or received lots of negative reinforcement, may need more time to heal. I spent much of my adult life recreating the abandonment patterns from my early childhood.

I was 5 years old when my father died in a plane crash. My mother went to work fulltime. I felt like I lost both parents. My siblings and I were left to take care of ourselves with no help for dealing with our loss.

Soon after that tragic day I closed my heart. I was incapable of emotional intimacy. It was not until my late forties that I even realized the depth of my trauma. I have spent the last 20 years on my own self-love journey.

My hope is that by engaging in the self-discovery and healing practices offered in this chapter, you will have more moments where you have the experience of loving all of yourself.

Self-Love Assessment

A deep understanding of the inner workings of our own minds enhances all personal and spiritual growth. So much of what runs us is not conscious. However, by noticing and tracking certain behaviors or patterns of behavior, we can gain clarity around what drives us, both positively and negatively.

To gauge your level of self-love, I invite you to take the following Self-Love Assessment. This assessment is based on observable behaviors that may relate to your level of confidence, which reflects your level of self-love. Each scenario assumes you are safe and that your action or response is appropriate and healthy in each situation.

The results of the test are only for you to see. So, think of this as an inner journey of discovery. Be kind and forgive yourself for any self-judgment that might arise.

INSTRUCTIONS: Quiet your mind and take three slow deep breaths. Feel into the space around your heart. Then read each sentence and circle the answer that feels most true.

NOTE: After deeply considering a certain question you may not be sure of your answer. This is possible in areas where you lack self-awareness. Skip those questions for now. Make a note of each question you skip and see if you notice those behaviors over the next few weeks. You can retake the test as often as you like to assess your improvement.

1) When I first meet someone, I easily smile and introduce myself.
a) Never b) Rarely c) Sometimes d) Often e) Always

2) I find it easy to say 'no' without explanation or any feeling of anxiety, angst, or guilt.
a) Never b) Rarely c) Sometimes d) Often e) Always

3 When someone pays me a compliment, I shrug it off or deflect it.
a) Never b) Rarely c) Sometimes d) Often e) Always

4) When someone points out a mistake I have made, I find ways to defend myself or prove that I am right – even if I am not.
a) Never b) Rarely c) Sometimes d) Often e) Always

5) When someone casually offers me advice, I am able to accept it graciously – even if it's something I already know.
a) Never b) Rarely c) Sometimes d) Often e) Always

6) When someone criticizes me without compassion, I feel angry, ashamed, or hurt.
a) Never b) Rarely c) Sometimes d) Often e) Always

7) When I sense people staring at me or talking near me, I assume they are thinking or saying something positive about me.
a) Never b) Rarely c) Sometimes d) Often e) Always

8) I am very comfortable with extended eye contact.
a) Never b) Rarely c) Sometimes d) Often e) Always

9) When something does not go the way I planned, I look for someone to blame.
a) Never b) Rarely c) Sometimes d) Often e) Always

10) When someone talks for an extended period of time, I feel the need to bring attention to myself.
a) Never b) Rarely c) Sometimes d) Often e) Always

Write you scores in the second column in the table below.

#	**Answer**	**Score**
Q1		
Q2		
Q3		
Q4		
Q5		
Q6		
Q7		
Q8		
Q9		
Q10		
Total		

Score each question using the following guidelines.

Scoring – Q1, Q2, Q5, Q7, Q8

a) 0
b) 2
c) 5
d) 8
e) 10

Scoring – Q3, Q4, Q6, Q9, Q10

a) 10
b) 8
c) 5
d) 2
e) 0

Once you have scored each question, find your total by summing all your scores.

Score: 0-39 – You may suffer from anxiety and experience a lot of stress and fear. Energetic healing and shadow work should be your main focus. Deep trauma clearing and family constellation work may be very helpful.

Score: 40-70 – While you may feel confident in some areas of your life, you may find yourself in fear and/or stressed in certain situations. Notice the areas where you feel less confident and focus on healing and shadow work in those areas. Deep trauma clearing and family constellation work may be helpful.

Score: 71-100 – You feel confident in most areas of your life. For further growth, take on challenges in areas where you feel less confident. Ask others for feedback around areas you can improve. Clearing trauma and blocking beliefs as well as family constellation work may be helpful.

Take a few minutes and reflect on your responses. See if you have any insights that might relate to current experiences you are having.

Roots of Self-Love

The following exercise is designed to help you see where you might have stuck energy from an early trauma or negative programming.

Take a few minutes and write some adjectives or words that describe your childhood within each age range. Feel free to list more if it is helpful. This exercise is for your eyes only.

Positive adjectives or descriptive words might include happy, safe, secure, loved, seen, attractive, valued, treasured, carefree, joyful, etc.

Negative adjectives or descriptive words might include lonely, lost, ashamed, unseen, worthless, ugly, hated, abused, terrified, abandoned, anxious, worried, etc.

It is common to have little to no recall from our earlier years, especially the years before age 6. If that is the case, perhaps you have a general sense of that period that could be described as positive or negative. If this applies to you, just write 'Positive' or 'Negative.' If you have no memories within any of these age ranges, this may indicate deeper trauma. In that case, just write 'No memory.'

Ages 0-2 __________ __________

__________ __________ __________

Ages 3-5 __________ __________

__________ __________ __________

Ages 6-12 __________ __________

__________ __________ __________

Age 13-21 __________ __________

__________ __________ __________

When you look at your adjectives for each age group, do you notice any patterns? Do you see any trends? Do you notice a point where the adjectives change from positive to negative or vice versa?

I spent a lot of my early life feeling sorry for myself. I had been on my own and emotionally shut down from a very early age. After many years of working alongside others on our healing journeys, I realized that I might be one of the lucky ones. For my first five years, I had a safe, nurturing, loving home. That foundation allowed me to access something in my healing journey that became an anchor for learning to love myself. Many others are not so lucky.

If you have many negative adjectives or if you are lacking memories for years 0-2, then your healing journey may be more challenging. Your feelings of loss or abandonment may be unconscious. These are often the most difficult to heal.

In the next section, we look at how our behaviors or reactions to our behaviors can provide clues to areas where healing is needed. Before you begin the next section, I invite you to take a few minutes to write down any thoughts you have or patterns you may have noticed about your adjectives in different age ranges.

Self-Mastery

Have you ever reacted to someone's behavior with feelings of anger or hurt? Have you ever been surprised by your own negative emotional response to a comment or action? Many refer to this as feeling 'triggered' or having our 'buttons pushed.' Sound familiar?

Self-mastery can also be thought of as mindfulness or self-awareness. When we are mindful and aware of ourselves, we are able to gracefully deal with difficult situations. On the other hand, our negative reactions and other behaviors offer clues to areas that may need healing.

For example, have you ever had a negative reaction when someone starts giving you unsolicited advice? While at the same time, do you enjoy giving advice to others? For most of us, our ego thoroughly enjoys being the expert and sharing our brilliance with others. When we are receiving advice, our ego can feel quite threatened and resentful.

I can share from personal experience that this was a hard lesson for me. This is because for most of my life, my emotions were unavailable. I survived almost exclusively using my intellect. I sought out an education that honed my quantitative skills, and I worked for companies in high-level positions solving complex problems.

Unfortunately, this behavior carried over into my personal life. My ego was fed by giving advice and solving everyone's problems. So if a friend came to me and needed to share something painful, I was ready with a solution. In fact, I became that dreaded friend that always offered advice. This came from a deep need to be valued and an inability to feel empathy. As I think back, I'm sure I annoyed a lot of people.

Many years ago, I was traveling with two friends. At that stage in my life, my ego was fed by offering unsolicited advice. I am sure I was over-bearing. A few days into the trip, one of my friends took me aside and said, "You really need to stop giving advice all the time." I said, "Why? Don't people want solutions?" She told me that people often do not want the answers to their problems. So, I asked her what to do if someone is complaining and I can see a clear solution. She said, "Ask that person if they want a suggestion." I thought this was brilliant, but it was not easy. I had to work hard at taming my impulse to fix everything. I had to be aware of that tendency and remember to wait and ask if they wanted a suggestion. But I was still missing a bigger lesson, one that came from a beloved family member.

One day my dear sister-in-law called me to catch up and share about a problem she was having. She was used to my habit of instantly offering solutions. So, before she started getting into her story she said, "Olivia, I don't want you to fix it. I just want you to listen!" I was shocked! For a couple of minutes, I wasn't sure what to do. My automatic reflex to offer a brilliant solution was no longer allowed! I remember being confused. I was thinking, well then why talk about it?

I gathered up my self-control and began to listen intently. I had to bite my tongue several times to keep from blurting out a solution. Soon, I started to see how just letting her talk was calming for her. I started to realize that my impulse to offer solutions might actually hinder her ability to process and find her own solutions. It was a real wake-up call for me.

Today, I still have a strong urge to fix people's problems. It's how I make my living! So, it's pretty hardwired. At the same time, I have become a much better listener. I purposely try to listen with compassion. And if I still feel the urge to offer a suggestion, I ask permission.

I also make an effort to understand people's styles and take clues from what they say and how they say it. I try to sense when someone wants my brilliant solutions (smile) and when someone simply wants to share. I have learned how to just stay quiet and give my full attention. I feel it is a gift to listen and just send love and light.

When we feel threatened, Eckhart Tolle says that our 'pain body' wakes up and tries to protect us from getting hurt. These reactions are common in areas where we have had trauma or have fears or negative beliefs about ourselves.

> *"The pain body wants to survive, just like every other entity in existence, and it can only survive if it gets you to unconsciously identify with it. It can then rise up, take you over, "become you," and live through you. It needs to get its "food" through you. It will feed on any experience that resonates with its own kind of energy, anything that creates further pain in whatever form: anger, destructiveness, hatred, grief, emotional drama, violence, and even illness." – Eckhart Tolle*

Becoming the Witness

Have you ever had one of those moments when you say something hurtful to someone and a little voice in your head says, "I can't believe I just said that." Do you have days when you can't seem to stop a destructive behavior, like eating junk food, even though you know it is not good for you?

I have done these behaviors more times than I would like to admit. Here is what I have learned: rather than beating yourself up, these are times when you must love yourself even more, especially those parts of yourself that you wish were different. I know it sounds simple. It is not always easy.

Experts say that 95 percent of our behaviors are driven by our unconscious mind. To master our thoughts and actions, we should be mindful of what is guiding our behavior in every moment.

I spent a large part of my life being a victim. I knew I was blaming others for everything that went wrong. After years of spiritual searching, it became so clear that everything is here to teach me and I have a choice in how I experience everything, positive and negative. In order to reach the point where you are responsible for your actions and create your own reality, you have to learn to be your own witness.

As your witness becomes active, you might say something that you know you will regret. The difference is that this time you are aware you are saying it while you are saying it! You might even think, "I can't believe I am saying this!" But somehow you can't seem to stop yourself. If you are smart, you will apologize and say that you didn't mean it.

The beauty of this is that if you have that awareness in the moment, you are fairly advanced along the path of mastering your thoughts and actions. Most of us have no idea what we are saying or its effect until we hear back from someone. And sadly, some people do not want to or are unable to give us constructive feedback. Instead, they can get triggered and react negatively or may begin to avoid contact with us altogether.

It can be challenging to master our thoughts and actions in every moment. Mastering our thoughts and actions means that we always anticipate the effect our words will have on others. It may sound simple but is far from easy. Every time you react with an angry comment or say something that you later regret, you are just beginning to master your thoughts and actions.

Before we review the levels, consider the following questions:

- Do you ever say something that you later regret saying?
- Are you ever surprised by other people's negative reactions?
- Do you find that certain people avoid getting into conversations with you?

I know some of these scenarios sound extreme. But we must look at any and all clues until we are able to track our own ability to master our thoughts and actions. If we feel really brave, we can also ask others for feedback. Consider asking a close friend the following:

- When I am talking to you, do you ever feel annoyed or frustrated?
- Do I have behaviors or lack behaviors that you find irritating or seem self-destructive?

Our ability to master our thoughts and actions may vary depending on our level of confidence in any given situation. When you read through these levels, think about different situations where you might be feeling more or less confident. This might inform how stressed or relaxed you are. We tend to be more impulsive and less aware of our thoughts when wc arc undcr stress.
Think about how much of your time is currently spent attempting to master your thoughts and actions.

Levels of Self-Mastery

As you embark on your path to self-mastery, the first step is to determine your dominant level, or the level at which you operate the majority of the time.

As you read through the levels, you might notice that it is not always a simple choice. Your level of self-mastery may vary depending on your situation. In other words, you might be in total control of your thoughts and actions when you are in certain places or with certain people, in situations where you feel confident and safe. Other places or people may cause you to be more reactive. I am always a little more reactive around family. Visiting family is one of the best ways for me to see where I need to do more of my own healing work.

Your level can even be affected by how you feel. I know that I am less in control of my actions and reactions when I have a headache or I am tired or hungry.

As you read through the levels of self-mastery and compare the behaviors to your own, notice if you find yourself at a certain level most of the time.

To assess your level or levels, read each statement aloud. See if you agree or disagree. Notice any feelings or sensations in your body. See if you can feel a resonance with one of the levels. Consider situations when you are not feeling your best. Notice if your behaviors are at a lower level.

Level 1 Statements:

“I say and do everything without regard for the consequences.”

“I have no idea how what I say or do affects other people.”

“Sometimes people respond negatively to me or avoid me all together and I have no idea why.”

Level 2 Statements:

“I often say or do things that I later regret.”

“When I notice that people are reacting negatively to me, I think about what I just said or did.”

“I often think to myself ‘I can’t believe I just said that’ or ‘I can’t believe I just did that.’”

Level 3 Statements:

"I often notice that I am saying or doing something *while* I am saying or doing it but still cannot stop myself, even though I know I will regret it later."

Level 4 Statements:

"I am often tempted to say or do things I will later regret and I am able to stop myself or change my behavior."

Level 5 Statements:

"I am rarely tempted to say or do things I will later regret."

Did you feel a resonance with one or two levels? Spend a few minutes writing down your thoughts. Then we will look at some strategies for getting to the next level.

Strategies for Self-Mastery

As you assess your level of self-mastery, you might notice that you are at different levels within different areas of your life. Depending on the area you want to improve, the following strategies offer suggestions for getting to the next level.

Level 1 Strategies:

If you are unaware of how your words or actions affect others and you really want to change, ask for feedback. If you feel up for it, ask your close friends to give you immediate feedback in a loving and compassionate way. If that is difficult, another method is to request that people in your tribe participate in a 360° Feedback – a process that provides structured anonymous feedback from people in all areas of your life. See the Resources section of the Appendix for more information.

As I shared earlier, I got some harsh feedback before I could stop myself from giving unsolicited advice. I am so grateful to those who had the courage to tell me and love me through it all. I now have friends who help me notice things I want to change.

Level 2 Strategies:

If you catch yourself after you say or do something you regret, the good news is that your witness is coming online. Take a deep breath to regain your center. Forgive yourself and remind yourself that you are doing your best. Then apologize to the affected person. If you feel comfortable, you can share that you do not like what happened, that you are working on changing, and that you would appreciate their understanding and compassion.

I remember being horrified and feeling physically ill when I linked my recent behavior to the experiences I was having with people. It was such a sinking feeling, and it still happens occasionally. It can still take some time for me to get past the self-admonishment to get to forgiveness. But, I eventually make it most of the time, and I apologize if possible. It is not always easy, but I find that it often helps the relationship. I have been amazed at how gracious people can be when I apologize from a deep and sincere place.

Level 3 Strategies:

If you catch yourself *while* saying or doing something you will regret, congratulations! Your witness is now working in real-time. Again, forgive yourself and remind yourself that you are doing your best. Then apologize to the affected person. If you feel comfortable, you can share that you are not happy about what happened, that you are working on changing, and that you would appreciate their understanding and compassion.

Sometimes I laugh when I realize that my behavior in the moment is regrettable. Usually I am eating food I should not eat. If I do not realize this until after I am done (level 2), my body reminds me in the morning.

I still say things I regret but do not often catch myself while I am saying them. I am working on getting better at that.

Level 4 Strategies:

If you are able to catch yourself before saying or doing something you know you will later regret, then your witness is fully online and working proactively. Congratulations! Celebrate this achievement! If you feel comfortable, share your successes with close friends.

Sink into and feel the joy of this achievement. This reinforces the behavior and reminds your brain that the behaviors you resisted are no longer wanted or needed. Eventually they will disappear.

While it is rare, I manage to catch myself sometimes, especially when I am interrupted while in a meeting or with a group. I take the interruption as a sign that perhaps I was not supposed to say what I was thinking. After reconsideration, I end up following through about half of the time. In the end I feel much more intentional.

Level 5 Strategies:

If behaviors you might regret are no longer showing up then it is really time to celebrate! Bask in the freedom of this level of self-mastery. If you want to grow from this level, spend time honing your intuition. With access to your higher guidance through your intuition, you can say or do anything without thinking and serve the greater good for everyone involved.

This is hard to for me to judge because it is the absence of something. What I have noticed is that I have fewer regrets overall. I see what I used to do that I do not do anymore. So, I know I am progressing.

Take a few minutes to reflect on your strategies and next steps.

Our Shadow

The following section is contributed by two brilliant and insightful women: Amy Myers and Bethany Rivett-Carnac. Amy and Bethany share my passion for healing and learning to love all of ourselves. In this section, they offer insights and strategies for embracing and integrating our negative side or shadow. You will notice some overlap with the concepts in the self-mastery work. In many ways, they reinforce each other.

Embracing Our Shadow

NOTE: The "I" voice in this section is Amy speaking.

We all have parts of us we don't like, that we wish were different. We wish we were better looking, smarter, stronger, less needy, less anxious, or more talented, etc. We all can relate. We are human. There are parts of us we like and parts we do not like.

There are times when we express the healthiest parts of ourselves and there are times when we express unhealthiest parts of ourselves. Sometimes we easily recognize our shadow sides and sometimes we do not recognize them at all. Sometimes we block them from our minds because they are too painful to see or we are too ashamed of them.

Carl Jung, one of the founders of modern psychology, first named the "shadow" as a part of all human beings. This was related to his concept of archetypes: patterns of being that exist deep within the collective unconscious of humanity and are common across all civilizations. And since his discovery, a number of archetype systems or ways to name archetypes have been developed. Each is based upon the premise that, while each of us is a unique being with a unique personality, we all collectively recognize and share these patterns simply because we are human.

For example, someone may manifest the ruler archetype when in charge of a team or an organization, bringing order to chaos, or establishing a system and way of doing things that allows for structured success. But this pattern of being also has a negative or shadow side: the ruler can be tyrannical, despotic, infatuated with power and control, and consequently, very frustrating or at worst a terror to others. Some of us may show up displaying the caretaker archetype when we make others feel supported and nurtured, which can be a wonderful gift to share in the world. The shadow of the caretaker, however, fails to practice self-care and hovers, if not dives altogether, into martyrdom, which then can lead to resentment against others for not reciprocating such sacrifice.

Jung's key idea is that we possess both the light and shadow within us, that we all have the capacity for good and bad thoughts, positive and negative acts, operating in healthy ways and unhealthy ways towards ourselves and others, and we have parts of ourselves we are proud of and other parts that we don't like or are even ashamed of. It is through fully understanding and accepting our whole self—a process Jung references as "individuation"—that we find our way to being at home in ourselves and can choose to live and express our best selves while accepting and loving all parts of ourselves.

A part of me that I do not like or one aspect of my shadow is my worrywart or nervous Nellie side. I try to control things because I do not want something bad to happen. I want it all to work out. At times I have overworked a problem or invested too much time in a project because I want to be sure it turns out right even if there are aspects I cannot control; I want to foresee all the risks and figure out how to take care of them even if it's impossible to plan for all risks. I am sure to some degree I internalized this from growing up in my family. Control was big in my house – everything had to be controlled and orderly. For example, friends could not just show up because things had to be picked up and look perfect. My mom wanted others to experience our home as neat and orderly. Also at times my dad was a worrier about life circumstances; while he and I laughed a lot and had lots of fun together, he had a side to him that sometimes seemed to assume the worst outcome from a situation – perhaps it was easier to assume the worst or worry about the worst scenario instead of taking the risk of being disappointed later on – a behavior I have seen in myself at times. As my dad lost his father at a very young age, perhaps he felt a loss of control and stability, and this contributed to what I sensed was a man who worried a lot.

Growing up my parents wanted the absolute best for me. My mom invested lots of time in my upbringing and got me involved in many activities all of which contributed significantly to my development in a positive way. However, this also meant that I did not have a childhood of play; I had a childhood of activities and achievement. At times, to this day my mom is sometimes unable to sit still – she seems anxious when she is not doing something. I do not like that side of my mom. I want to be different and yet I also have a hard time sitting still sometimes. I express this same need to constantly do or achieve. My inability to slow down, this overachiever, is also a part of my shadow.

Then there are those times when my husband calls me out on certain tendencies to deflect in our conversations. In those moments I see a side of myself I am not always aware of and do not really want to see. Whether originating from our mom's, our dad's, our siblings, early life experiences or just innate qualities, these darker aspects exist in all of us.

Some of my dark sides are: worrier, negative Nellie, *needy* Amy, *shy girl, victim, elitist smart girl, goody two shoes, rules follower to-a-tee, over-achiever, interrupter, constant doer, controller. These all exist within me just like all the great parts of me exist too.*

Many of us feel these sides of ourselves need to be fixed. We see these as our problems or imperfections. Or we just don't want to see them and push them away or repress them. And yet these are simply part of who we are as human beings. As Carl Jung acknowledged: "I would rather be whole than good." We see his powerful contribution to the human experience today as more societal leaders, psychologists, and spiritual teachers advocate that accepting all sides of ourselves leads us to greater self-acceptance and inner peace. This self-acceptance frees our energy to focus on how we want to be in the world, and how we can express our full creativity instead of worrying about fixing those sides of ourselves that may just continue to be a part of us during this lifetime. There is that notion that "what we resist, persists", which suggest that the more we try to neglect or deny our dark sides, the more we will have to fight. Some would say that our lives are a journey to learn to love all parts of ourselves.

Why love our dark sides? Love them because we all have them. Love them because they are simply a part of us. Being human means, we have all sides to us – the light, the dark, and many shades of gray. The good, the bad, the ugly, the neutral, and the amazing.

When we identify and connect with our shadow sides along with all the amazing parts of ourselves, we can begin a healing process that allows our shadow to be acknowledged, understood, and loved while we have more ability to live as our healthiest and best selves. When we continue to repress or be blind to these aspects of ourselves, our shadow sides may have more control over our feelings, our actions, and how we are living. Whereas when we accept and love all of ourselves, we can work with, manage, and moderate these sides of ourselves in a more helpful way. This gives us a greater ability to make healthy choices along with a greater ability for self-empathy, self-compassion, and growth.

I realized the power of this self-acceptance and self-forgiveness when I healed from my first chronic pain experience. There were aspects of my past and present that I was not fully embracing, and ways I was being in the world that I did not really like or even want to see. There were needs I had that went against how I wanted others to see me or how I felt I should be to be successful in society. I needed to simply see these aspects of myself and be okay with them. This helped me heal from chronic pain as a from a year and a half of debilitating symptoms heading me towards possible life in a wheelchair. This was clearly a sign to me that something was not working, that I needed to get in touch with all of myself, learn to fully appreciate all of myself and all of my needs. Once I did this, my health returned rapidly and I was back to my fully active self while continuing on the journey of learning about all of me and loving all of me.

Getting in touch with all sides of ourselves, including our shadow sides, allows us to fully love ourselves, not just the parts that we believe society will accept. When we do this, we unleash our full creativity and brilliance into the world. We allow any energy that we were using to suppress what we did not like or did nor even want to see, to instead fuel us in the full expression of our gifts, to support us in enjoying a life of wholeness, and a life of being at peace with all aspects of ourselves. This also gives us permission to forgive ourselves for when we hit road bumps along the way, make mistakes, or do things we think we should not do. It also unleashes a deeper sense of compassion for those around us, even those who trigger and frustrate us. We suddenly realize that we all have our dark and bright sides and it is simply a part of the human experience.

Part of my journey has been to forgive myself when I cannot slow down, when I always feel like I need to be doing or achieving. This has also led me to forgive my mom for this part of her that I naturally internalized from being her daughter. I admire the beautiful side of the achiever in my mom, the side that has given her the courage to travel the world by herself many times, the side of her that has endless energy to take care of whatever needs taking care of, the side of her that is so active in her seventies and an inspiration to many with her daily commitment to Zumba and her certification as a Zumba instructor and her active role across the global Zumba community. At the same time, I can forgive her and love her for those human moments when her zest for achievement does not want to slow down.

I can see into myself more fully and forgive myself when my Nervous Nellie side takes over or when that side that wants nothing to go wrong but is always fearful that something might. And I can see how that risk identifier in my dad that forecasts all possible pitfalls has translated into a conscientiousness that has been a huge contributor to my success in life while I also see the worried side of my dad for what is it, simply his worried side. It doesn't have to trigger me as much as it once did. I love and admire him just as he is.

Thanks to wonderful people in my life including an amazing therapist, and two wonderful coaches as well as amazing authors and teachers who have written about the Shadow extensively such as Debbie Ford with her The Dark Side of the Light Chasers book, I have experienced some powerful healing in befriending my shadow. Because of this powerful work, I can love all of myself while having the full autonomy and ability to choose to live from the healthiest and most brilliant parts of me while continuing to grow and discover more amazing parts of myself. I also find that as I learn to know and accept aspects of my Shadow more and more, similar aspects in others are less triggering, giving me more capacity for connection and full acceptance of others just the way they are.

So how do we get in touch with these aspects of ourselves that we can see but just do not like as well as the aspects of ourselves that we do not or cannot even see?

Once we get in touch with them, what do we do with them? How do we make peace with them? How do we learn to love them so we can fully love ourselves?

To name those shadow sides that we are aware of reflect on the following questions:

- When I am feeling low or stressed, what aspects of me come out?
- What am I aware of about myself that may be challenging for others?
- What am I often embarrassed by in myself?
- What do I not want to tell others or what do I hide from others because I am worried they won't accept me?

To uncover those shadow sides of yourself that may be hidden, that you may be less aware of, or that you at times are blocking from your awareness:

1) Seek out friends and family members with whom you comfortable and safe to ask for feedback. Ask them two simple questions:
   - What shows up when I show up? What wonderful qualities do I bring into the room when I show up?

- What sides of me do you see when I am in a stressful situation? What sides of me do you see when I am not at my best?

2) Consider what bothers you or triggers you in reaction to other people.

____
____
____
____
____
____
____
____
____
____
____
____
____
____

Many psychologists, human development leaders, and spiritual teachers have expressed the idea that what we do not like in others is something we do not like in ourselves. While we may look at someone else and think they are lazy and look down on them, there is most likely some lazy part in ourselves that we are not fully embracing. Consider again Carl Jung's theory of archetypes and the collective unconscious which espouses that as human beings we all share these universal patterns of being that make us human. Jung describes archetypal patterns that have both light and dark qualities. It makes sense that we are naturally triggered by those aspects of others that we do not want to see in ourselves but most likely exist in some form in ourselves. In essence, others serve as a mirror for us to know our own selves better. Consider the following questions and see what surfaces within you.

- What advice do I give to others that when I think about it often applies to me?
- What aspects of others do I get most frustrated by that I can see in myself?

Our early experiences in life shape us including both the amazing brilliant qualities that reside within us and also the darker more challenging qualities that reside within us. We are aware of the impact of some of our early life experiences, and the impacts of some may not be fully visible to us. This next exercise helps you get in touch with experiences that may have shaped some aspects of your Shadow and then based on those experiences, it helps you connect into these darker aspects of yourself.

Consider that you may want to complete each step one at a time, allowing yourself space in between for reflection. This may bring up difficult aspects of your experience, things that make you feel bad; you may want to ensure you are in a comforting and supportive space, both physically and emotionally – when you work through this exercise:

- Write down everything that makes you angry or sad related to your parents and early upbringing as well as present situation. It does not matter how you write it down, just make an inventory – it could be a long narrative or just a list. What's most important is that it feels deeply true for you.
- Step back and review everything you wrote down.
    - What insights do you have about these aspects of your experience growing up, as well as any aspects of your present situation that you identified?
    - What do you sense has been their impact on you?
    - How do these experiences manifest in how you feel sometimes, in how behave or operate towards yourself, towards others? How do you show up sometimes as a result of these experiences?
- Review what you have uncovered and complete the phrases with the Shadow aspects you can start to see in yourself:
    - My parents raised a daughter/son who..... (e.g. always wants to control the outcome, feels the need for constant validation, must be the life of the party even if that means totally dominating a conversation, feels like he wants to disappear as soon as the spotlight is cast on me)
    - I grew up as a person who.... (e.g. who must be right and needs to tell others why they are wrong, who wants to chill out and procrastinates on getting necessary things done sometimes,

wants to win at all costs, feels left out if I am not constantly involved with what's going on, etc.)

Now that you have identified these aspects of yourself, my dear business partner and soul sister, Beth, offers up how you can learn to essentially dance with your shadow so that you can fully acknowledge it, be okay with it, and have the capacity to live from the best parts of yourself.

Dancing with the Shadow

NOTE: The "I" voice in this section is Bethany speaking.

Growing up I had parents who always encouraged me to 'just to do my best'. They did not push me to achieve particularly, but were encouraging of me choosing the things I most enjoyed and pursue those. This served me well in many ways; I felt supported to take time off before committing to University so I could figure out what I enjoyed, and also to ease the pressure off needing certain grades to get a specific place at University. They supported me heading off to travel alone during my year off despite their fears as parents, and as a result of this freedom I was able to choose what felt good to me. Choosing my career path became an exercise in self-exploration, rather than needing to meet any external expectations put on me. As I look at the shadow side of my independent spirit I see that there are times when I rebel against doing things I do not want to do, even when they will help me achieve great things. I also do not find it easy to set goals for myself, which can mean that I sometimes lack direction and focus. I have noticed that this desire for freedom that I was able to nurture and express can sometimes mean I get bored easily and resist being 'boxed in' or reap the benefits of some structure. This can manifest in quite a bit of chaos in my way of working and even in completing administrative tasks that I feel are too process orientated.

Another curious thing I have noticed is that some of my shadow elements can seem in contradiction to each other. Growing up, I was surrounded by a large extended family; many of my cousins and I are quite close in age. Naturally, there were some comparisons. One particular aunt was incredibly proud of the achievements of her children and she was very vocal about this. I have noticed that I have a paradox within me. Sometimes I want to be boastful of my achievements to satisfy my desire to be outwardly celebrated in the way I saw my cousins being celebrated while they were growing up. Also, I am incredibly resistant to owning and sharing my strengths with others, for fear of being boastful. This paradox can mean that I sabotage and fail to acknowledge and celebrate my successes, or rely on others' praise to make me feel good enough.

'Both light and shadow are the dance of Love' – Rumi

The Dance of Love

Now that you have done the work of the Heart Warrior to identify the shadow elements of yourself, we invite you to join us in an exercise of celebration. In the exercise 'The Dance of Love', you will not only accept each of the aspects you have identified as part of you alongside your strengths, but you will take it one step further and shine the light of love onto them in celebration.

Time

This exercise works best when you create a beautiful, comfortable space for it and gift yourself the time.

Choose a time when you can work uninterrupted by outside demands for your time and attention. Set aside an hour just for you.

Space

We also recommend creating the environment that speaks of the heart work you are about to do.

We hope you will accept our invitation to choose a space that feels sacred to you, or you can add some personal touches to help you tune out of everyday life, and tune in to yourself. Perhaps this space is a snug corner of your house, with fresh flowers, your favorite music and a couple of candles. Maybe, for you, some time in your favorite natural environment makes you feel most at home. For some, this work can be a beautiful addition to a long soak in the bath.

What you will need

The list of shadows and strengths you have identified.

A journal and pen handy to capture any insights from the exercise.

Now you have the time and space: It is time to dive in.

Imagine you are standing before the closed door of a large room. Behind the door, you can sense that it is full of vibrancy and fun. You hear your favorite music playing inside and can hear the sounds of joy coming from behind the doors.

You realise very quickly that inside there is a party going on and as you look at the sign on the door and realize it is called 'Life'.

With your hand on the doorknob, you decide to enter.

As you open the door, you look around and notice that the people in this room are all different versions of you. Each person illustrates a characteristic or persona you identified as you bring to mind your strengths and shadows.

You enter the room and are greeted immediately with the persona who you recognize as the blocker of fun and joy, the part of you that most gets in the way of all of you experiencing the best time you could have in the party of life. It is the inner party pooper within you.

You give this persona a name that captures the characteristics or traits they encapsulate. Perhaps something along the lines of 'Self Doubt Sally' or 'Jackass Jock'.

Jot that down in your journal now alongside the description.

As you come eye to eye with this part of you, you notice how this version of you carries itself. You observe the body language, facial expressions and movement. You notice how, if at all, they are dancing to the music. You make a note of what you notice now and a catchphrase that you are most likely to hear coming from them.

If you fancy getting artistic with this exercise, you could always choose to do a simple drawing of this persona. This is an image just for you (it doesn't have to be perfect).

You also observe how this part of you interacts with other characters in the room. Notice if there are any personas in particular whose enjoyment of the party are helped or hindered most from its presence.

As you observe this character in action, now you tune into its behavior and look for the unmet need behind that behavior. Find the thing that would allow that part of you to enjoy the party of life more.

Perhaps in the case of 'Self Doubt Sally' it is a need to be reassured and let her hair down. For 'Jackass Jock', it is a need to be noticed and a desire for some fun company.

You feel for the origin of that need; perhaps it was inherited from behaviors that persona had seen modelled for them growing up, a particular life event that led to that persona showing up, or maybe it is purely an inner emotion. You ask your compassionate persona in the room to send a beam of love to the original cause of that need.

Now, you get to work meeting the needs of that part of you, using any of the other personas in the room to help you if you like.

You witness the transformation occur as this part of you has its needs met and starts to enjoy the party. You notice the way the body language shifts and you hear the laughter as they celebrate with you.

With this part of you now thoroughly enjoying the party, you bring to mind one of the other personas you feel drawn to meet. Maybe it is the rebellious you, the cynical you, or even the dramatic you.

Repeat the steps above:

Observe: Its behavior, the way it carries itself, what you hear and feel most from them, and how it interacts with other parts of you.

Identify: Where this part of you originated, what triggers this part of you to show up in your life, and what this part needs from you now.

Embrace and Transform: Allow yourself to meet the needs of this persona, or speak to this part of you. Invite it to transform and meet other parts of you that will help it to join you in celebrating and enjoying itself.

You can choose to work your way through each of your personas one by one. As you become aware of these aspects of yourself, you can add them to the party scene.

When you notice one of the personas you have cared for through this exercise showing up in your life, you have the invitation to greet them like an old friend, meet their needs, and observe with curiosity what a difference that makes. You might even find that you begin to get a deeper understanding of their (aka YOUR) needs and you may find an opportunity moment by moment to meet them.

Acts of Self-Love

Over the last 30 years, I have made my healing and transformational work a priority in my life. I have worked with shamans, spiritual masters, and various healers. I have attended a multitude of personal growth workshops and healing seminars.

What follows are some of my favorite exercises. I invite you to delve in and explore where you can take steps to discover what limits you from being your most amazing self, as well as where you can love all of yourself even more.

Affirmations

Early in my healing journey I was introduced to the concept of affirmations. I attended a half-day workshop during which the facilitator described a very simple theory: that most of our negative actions and reactions are driven by subconscious beliefs or wounds from early trauma. As I looked at my own behavior, this made perfect sense to me.

The facilitator then claimed that if we commit to listening to affirmations for 30 minutes a day for 30 days, we can overwrite any negative beliefs in our subconscious mind. He said that deeper wounds may take longer to heal. But if we work on negative beliefs, we could eliminate 70-75 percent or our negative behavior. As a researcher, I was intrigued.

So what exactly are **affirmations**? Simply put, **whatever we say or think to ourselves** is an affirmation. All of your self-talk, or the dialogue in your head, is a stream of affirmations. Words other people say to you about yourself that you accept as true become affirmations.

You might shrug off negative self-talk or comments from others. But affirmations are messages that lodge in your subconscious mind. Over time, these messages can inform and establish habitual ways of thinking and behaving.

The act of reading, listening to, or speaking positive affirmations out loud plants healing thoughts and ideas deep into our consciousness that support us in developing self-confidence and healthy self-esteem. The result is our ability to remain calm in stressful situations. As we heal, we experience more joy and peace of mind. Eventually, we feel free to take risks and show up fully as the greatest expression of ourselves.

In LOVE@WORK, *The Essential Guide to a Life of Inspired Purpose*, I share my story about remapping my entire brain by listening to positive affirmations while I slept. This nightly practice was a powerful early step in my healing journey. I highly recommend it to anyone who has negative self-talk or self-destructive thoughts or behaviors.

Back in the early nineties, I developed a regular practice. Each night I would put my positive affirmations tape into my cassette player. I would pop on headphones and fall asleep listening to sentences like: "I love myself." "You love yourself." "My friends love me." "Your friends love you." It sounded silly at the time, but I was determined to give it a chance. I fell asleep quickly and listened for a few hours.

After about 3 weeks, I began to notice that I was reacting differently to people. I was much less defensive. I got very excited. This was really working! I immediately thought, "What else could I program?" I sought out other positive messages and used them for the next 6-7 years almost every night.

Let's look at some strong positive affirmations. Then we will explore other powerful ways to use them:

"I am lovable."
"I love myself."
"My family loves me."
"My friends love me."
"I am brilliant."
"I am a valuable member of society."
"I deserve abundance."
"I am strong."
"I am fearless."
"I am totally at peace with myself."

"When I fully express myself, I am safe."
"By doing my best, I inspire others to do their best."
"I am open to abundance."
"I have plenty of time to get everything done."
"My work is valued in the world."
"I have the courage to be the greatest version of myself."

In addition to listening to affirmations while you sleep, affirmations can be posted in strategic places around your home or work area (when appropriate). Posting notes on your bathroom mirror or on your computer monitor help to make them visible.

Placing affirmations on your mirror invites a deeper dive into healing.

Mirror Work with Affirmations

*"**Mirror work** is the most effective method I've found for learning to love yourself and see the world as a safe and loving place."* - Louise Hay

The most powerful affirmations are those you say out loud when you are in front of your mirror looking into your own eyes. Why?

When you look into your own eyes and say something positive to yourself, you can feel if it does not ring true. The mirror always reflects back the feelings you have about yourself.

I remember the first time I looked at myself in the mirror, I mean really looked into my own eyes. I was in my fifties! I could barely maintain eye contact! I tried saying "I love you" to myself. It was so difficult. In addition to this being hard to say, it was difficult to receive it from myself. It took many months of daily affirmations and mirror work before I was able to look at myself and not cringe. It was years before I could really feel love for myself.

As you begin to do mirror work, you will become much more aware of the words you say and the things you do. At least once a day, look at yourself in the mirror and say something nice like "Thank you!" or "You are amazing." Say the same thing every day for a week and notice if it gets easier.

If you are having a bad day, try going to the mirror and saying, "It's okay. You are doing your best. You will get through this. You are strong."

Eventually, you will become very comfortable with your mirror dialogue. You might even look forward to it! Ultimately, if we want to love all of ourselves, we must fall in love with our reflection. It will always respond in kind and with kindness.

Receiving and Allowing

How do you respond when someone compliments you? For most of my life, I was unable to receive complements. On a very deep level and without realizing it, I didn't feel deserving.

Our ability to receive praise is highly correlated with our level of self-love. A great technique for improving our ability to receive is to ask a friend to participate in a little role-play.

Invite your friend (or group of friends) to sit on a chair facing you. You stand facing your friend from 4-5 feet away. Ask your friend to tell you things they like about you. Ask them to use "I" messages. "I like this about you." or "I admire you when you do this or that." Request that they not use "You are this or that." This is received by your brain as that friend being in a position of authority. Rather, you want them to state their opinion using 'I' messages.[1]

Your role is to stand with your arms by your side and your palms facing forward. This puts you in a posture to receive. While your friend is complimenting and praising you, try to stand very still and maintain eye contact. Your only task is to say, "Thank you, I know" after each compliment. This may feel very awkward and uncomfortable. Just try it anyway as a practice to stretch your ability to receive.

Out in the real world, we can practice just saying "Thank you." I realize that this might sound simple. But it is not always easy. I found it so difficult the first time I tried it. I wanted to make excuses about why I was not deserving of any kind of praise. I still sometimes catch myself deflecting praise. It is a constant practice to remember to just smile and say, "Thank you."

Forgiving Ourselves and Others

A big part of loving ourselves is being able to forgive ourselves and others. Let's start with forgiving others.

"Holding a grudge is like drinking poison and hoping the other guy will die." – Original Source Unknown2

Forgiving Others

Is there anyone in your life against whom you have held a grudge for many years? Take a couple minutes and think. Is there anyone you are still angry with for any reason?

Forgiving those who have hurt you is simultaneously one of the most difficult and most freeing actions you can take. Forgiving someone does not mean that you no longer hold them accountable for what they did to you. It just means that you are letting go of the stuck energy in your body where the anger or grudge resides. It is really good for *your* health!

"The practice of forgiveness is our most important contribution to the healing of the world."
- Marianne Williamson

I embrace the philosophy that the only failure in life is the failure to learn. So even the worst actions against me happened to teach me something. In that context, I can not only forgive someone who hurt me but I can also thank them for the experience.

Most of us have done things that we regret. While there are people with hostile intentions, most people are trying to do their best.

"Everything we do is either an act of love or a cry for help."
- Marianne Williamson ~

Many times, those who hurt us are acting out as the result of their own wounds. If we can feel compassion for them, it can help us find it in our hearts to forgive them.

The beautiful thing about forgiveness work is that you do it by yourself. You do not need to interact with the person who harmed you. They never need to know that you forgave them. This is purely for your benefit.

I invite you to think of someone towards whom you still feel anger or resentment. This person can be alive or dead. Close your eyes.

Take three deep breaths. Picture this person sitting somewhere. It could be in front of you, or in their home, or somewhere that you last remember seeing them. Feel into your heart space and imagine connecting to their heart space. See them in your mind's eye and say, "I forgive you." You do not even have to mean it or feel it. Just imagine saying it and then let go. Take another deep breath and say it again, "I forgive you."

At this point, you may start to feel a shift towards compassion. If not, that is okay. Do not try to force it. Open your eyes and notice if you feel differently towards that person.

Forgiving Ourselves

Have you ever beaten yourself up mercilessly for a stupid mistake or comment? I have done this more times than I want to admit.

As a child, I tried to get attention by being funny. So I developed a quick wit, which served me well for many years. I was able to connect with humor and sarcasm while keeping my heart tightly shut.

Today, I rarely engage in sarcasm. I still enjoy humor if it is not at the expense of others. But I occasionally let something slip that I later regret. Or I will say something in a meeting that does not come out right, so I think everyone sees me as stupid. After my initial self-judgment, I have learned to forgive myself.

Forgiving others is easy compared to forgiving ourselves. If we grow up hearing negative messages, we can be hard on ourselves. Sound familiar?

I invite you to think of something you said or did that you still regret. Or perhaps there is something that you wish you had said or done but did not. Regrets for not taking action can be just as painful.

Can you be comfortable knowing that you were doing your best? What can you imagine a dear friend telling you? I have a wonderful friend who I can call when I become very self-critical. She always helps me see my own heart and intentions. If we are on a healing path, we are all doing the best we can.

Extreme Self-Care

The depth to which we love ourselves is often reflected in our level of self-care. With our busy lives, we may find it challenging to eat well, get enough exercise and sleep, and find time for play and relaxation.

This area is particularly challenging for me. I am unmasking my own deep programming that says I cannot relax until I get everything done. I often find it hard to leave my phone and computer and go for a walk or meditate. And yet I know both of these activities will give me more energy to get things done. I am currently using the affirmation, "I have plenty of time to get everything done."

As we become more dependent on technology, our way to escape may take us in the opposite direction. According to Martha Beck, "The scarcest, most coveted resources aren't high-tech machines or highly developed cities, but "unspoiled" places, people, animal, objects, and experiences."[3]

There is increasing evidence that what we put into our bodies has serious long-term effects on our health. Yet with our busy lives, it can be challenging to eat well all the time. In my experience, the more we support ourselves with natural food, the better our health will be.

A huge component of self-care is having friends that support us. As we heal and deepen in our self-love, we may find that some of our friends and family members no longer support our growth. We do not have a choice to change families. But we can find new friends. This is very important if we want to continue to heal and live with an open heart.

Spending time with our family of origin can still be powerful. We just need to set our expectations, or rather drop any expectations. Interacting with parents and siblings can be a great way to see what areas still need healing.

After many years of working with my own affirmations, I started spending more time with my siblings. This was when I realized I still had a lot of work to do. At first I was shocked at how reactive

I was. Then I felt grateful for the opportunity to see more places where I needed to love myself.

I invite you to go to the Appendix and take the Self-Care Assessment. Notice the places where you may be out of balance in your life. Take small steps each day or week to improve your self-care. Celebrate each improvement!

Healing Tools and Techniques

When seeking professional help for our self-healing, most of us are encouraged to pursue talk therapy. And while it can be very healing to talk about our issues, unless we access our emotional body and our energy body, the deeper issues will not surface. If trauma is very deep, talk therapy can take years or a lifetime and still not lead to healing. Trauma is an energy that is stored in the body. Trauma is often accompanied by memories. But the deepest trauma may not be recognized by the left brain, so only talking may never access unconscious memories.

Gestalt Therapy can be a powerful technique for healing trauma. But it is often limited by what we remember. Another drawback of Gestalt Therapy is that it directs us to recreate the experience, which may be healing but also has the potential to retraumatize us.

Fortunately, there are several somatic healing modalities that work with a combination of our physical bodies and our energy bodies to facilitate the healing of trauma at all levels. If you have deep trauma, whether it is conscious or unconscious, I invite you to explore any or all of the following:

Breathwork covers a range of therapies that utilize breathing exercises to improve mental, emotional, and physical health. Breathwork draws from many traditions including yoga and Tai Chi, and some standard psychotherapy techniques like art, music, bodywork and talk therapy.[4]

Somatic Therapy is also known as Body Oriented Psychotherapy. The goal is to help the mind and body communicate with the goal of releasing trauma or improving emotional health.[5]

Energy Psychology is an approach to emotional and physical healing that uses bioenergy systems.[6] Using muscle testing, acupressure points, affirmations, visualizations, and other techniques, energy psychology addresses the underlying energetic aspects of the problem. The specific energy psychology that I have used extensively is **CLEAR®.** I was first introduced to it in 2000. I still use it every day.

Family Constellation is a healing process that uses the energy of the family system (or other system) to break patterns of anger, guilt, loneliness, alcoholism, and even illness that we take on to connect and ease suffering in our family. The resulting shifts in the system can free us to live happier, healthier lives. I have done over 50 family constellations and feel they are one of the most powerful healing processes available today.[7]

There are other ways to clear trauma and facilitate healing. I encourage you to try these or do your own research around healing trauma.

Final Thoughts

I strongly suggest that our capacity to love all of ourselves is essential to thrive in the new world we are creating. I feel that love is foundational for both business success and personal happiness.

As we move ahead in our lives and our careers, we must all think of ourselves as leaders. Complexity is increasing in every area of our lives. To manage this complexity, we have to work together to co-create the results we want to see. To effectively work together, we must build connection and trust. This is best built on a foundation of self-love.

STEP 2: OWN YOUR SUPERPOWERS

When you think of your favorite superhero, what qualities or skills come to mind? I often think I would love to be able to fly like Superman, or to disappear, like the Invisible Man. Have you ever had the desire to make yourself invisible? Alas, many of these are unrealistic for us mere mortals.

Fortunately, many of us do have untapped superpowers, that if discovered and nurtured can bring benefit to the world. If this resonates with you then I invite you to take this journey of self-discovery.

Self-Inquiry

The most common ego identifications have to do with possessions, the work you do, social status and recognition, knowledge and education, physical appearance, special abilities, relationships, person and family history, belief systems, and often nationalistic, racial, religious, and other collective identifications. None of these is you. – Eckhart Tolle

In an effort to unveil and identify your superpowers, try the following simple exercise. In preparation, have a pen and paper or your favorite journal handy to capture your ideas, insights, and feelings.

TIP: Our left brains love to make us right. If you feel blocked or this exercise feels difficult, just say out loud, "I can't believe how easy it is to discover my superpowers." It may feel very artificial to say this. Do it anyway. The results may amaze you!

Sit in a quiet place. To help quiet your mind, focus on your breathing. Take a few slow deep breaths. Speaking softly ask yourself the question, "Who am I?" Repeat this question at least 10 times with a few seconds between. Write down any thoughts that come into your head.

When I first did this exercise, I started hearing the standard identifiers that I typically use to describe myself. "I am a mom." "I am a data scientist." "I am a spiritual seeker." As I kept asking, new descriptors started popping into my head. "I am a cancer survivor." "I am a problem solver." "I am a whole-brain thinker." "I am an activist." "I am a writer."

As I jotted down my insights, I began to see how my self-descriptors were clues to my superpowers. Take a few minutes and write down any words that identify you in the world.

In LOVE@WORK, *The Essential Guide to a Life of Inspired Purpose*, I list some superpowers that are common to those of us who are seeking purpose and meaning in our lives. See if any of these qualities feel natural to you:

- Empathic (nurse, childcare worker, hospice worker, leader, healer)
- Deep listener (psychotherapist, coach, hospice worker, healer)
- Sees potential greatness in others (teacher, coach, manager, leader)
- System thinker (CEO, engineer, politician)
- Intuitive and sensitive (healer, coach, artist)
- Problem solver (analyst, consultant)
- Artistically gifted (artist, musician, designer)

Anchor Your Joy

Can you remember times in your life when you felt pure joy? Do you recall moments, perhaps in your childhood, when you felt blissfully happy?

Feeling joy offers clues to our deepest yearnings. As an adult, that feeling of pure joy may seem rare. I invite you to try a little exercise.

Sit in a quiet place and close your eyes. Take three slow, deep breaths. Recall a time in your life when you felt joy. Go back as far as you need to go. In your mind's eye, picture what you are doing. See if you can get that feeling in your body. Feel the joy resonating through your body. Spend a few minutes recalling and feeling this joy.

Keep your eyes closed and using your mind's eye, take a look around. Where are you? What are you doing? Try to notice every detail. Open your eyes and write about your experience.

I had a client who during this exercise found herself sitting in a forest surrounded by children. At the time, she was working in a hospital, so she loved being outdoors. The vision brought her so much joy that she decided to volunteer at a camp with the goal of starting her own camp for children.

Another client was a psychologist who had a love of art and design. During this exercise, she found herself in a conference room sharing her designs. She decided to pursue a career in sales and marketing that expressed her love of design while leveraging her psychology background.

Find Your Flow

Have you ever been so engrossed in a project that you lost track of time? Have you ever noticed that you are feeling unusually calm and everything seems to synchronize perfectly and effortlessly? Notice what you are doing, because these may be indications that you are in flow.

For the next week, pay attention to times when you feel you are in flow, and feeling very creative. Notice what comes naturally to you. Notice the activities you are drawn to without thinking or planning. Keep a log of these times noting the time of day, what you were doing, and how you felt.

If you are not sure when you are in creative flow, try to notice when you lose track of time, or perhaps when you are feeling especially content. I often feel this when I am involved in an art project or coaching a client.

Many years ago, I was working at a credit card bank that was being acquired by another bank where I had worked previously. Because of my knowledge of the other bank, I ended up coaching my fellow workers. The fact that I felt so much more gratified at the end of the day told me that I was in flow when I was coaching.

Another client with a stressful corporate career tracked her flow for a week. She discovered that her greatest flow was while she was doing yoga. She spent the next year cutting back her corporate work and trained to become a yoga teacher.

Your Most Admired List

Thinking about people you admire helps you to unveil, clarify and own your superpowers. This practice can also start to unveil your inspired purpose. Ask yourself the following questions:

Whom do I admire?

What are the qualities or activities that you admire about them?

Which of these qualities do you have within yourself?

Which of their activities would you like to be doing?

What we admire about others are often latent qualities or yearnings within ourselves. Repeat this exercise every few weeks. Pay attention to whom you are drawn in the media. Notice if new yearnings or admirable qualities emerge. These are clues to your Superpowers.

Feedback from Others

A powerful way to learn about yourself and unveil your Superpowers is to request feedback from others. This exercise is similar to the 360° feedback exercise mentioned in the Self-Mastery section of Step 1: Love All of Yourself. The main difference is it focuses more on your strengths, gifts, and talents and is limited to positive feedback.

To get started, ask your closest friends to give you a list of what they see as your strengths, gifts, and talents. Let them know that you just want positive responses. I think you will be amazed at how people see you, especially in ways that you do not see yourself.

A fun group exercise is what is known as a "Strength Shower." Or I call it a "Love Shower." It is really simple. You can do it with friends or acquaintances. Get into groups of two to four people. Here is how it works:

Each person takes 10-15 minutes to write 5-10 (agree on the number ahead of time) positive characteristics about all other members in the group. Next, you pick someone be the first person to receive. Let's say that is you. One at a time, each group member shares with you their list of what they like or admire about your gifts and talents. Once everyone has read you their lists, you move to the next person.

If you are with someone you do not know well, you can always find positive things to say to someone you just met like "I like your smile" or "You feel like a kind person."

This exercise can break through barriers and allow for deep connection with others in your group. Sounds like fun, doesn't it? And you will learn all sorts of things about yourself.

After you complete the process, write down some of your feelings. Feel into the joy of being truly seen, heard, and valued… i.e. **loved**.

Gratitude for Your Superpowers

To be yourself in a world that is constantly trying to make you into something else is the greatest accomplishment. – Ralph Waldo Emerson

At this point, you should have a decent list of superpowers. Write them on the lines below. Do not be shy. Go for it!

NOTE: If you feel resistant to making this list because it feels like you are being boastful, remember that you are stepping up in service of the greater good. And you do not have to share this list with anyone. If you still cannot write out your list of superpowers, go back to Step 1: Love All of Yourself. Repeat the affirmation, "I am grateful for my talents and gifts. I use my gifts in service of the greater good."

Once you have made your list of superpowers, go back through the list. After each superpower, write how it serves you and others. Feel into each one for a couple minutes. Know that these are your innate gifts that the world needs you to share.

Work on this list a little every day. You will be amazed at how long it can get!

Final Thoughts

Once you have your list of superpowers, spend a little time thinking about how the qualities in this list have been present throughout your life. Many of our superpowers are talents that helped us survive difficult situations and brought us to where we are today. This path of struggle and learning is shaping our journey to discover our inspired purpose and take our gifts or superpowers into the world. In Step 3: Visualize Your Inspired Purpose, we will fine-tune our path and bring our life into focus.

STEP 3: VISUALIZE YOUR INSPIRED PURPOSE

"Whatever you can do, or dream you can, begin it. Boldness has genius, power and magic in it."
~ Goethe

Is there anything in your life about which you feel most passionate? Is there a topic you always want to be discussing?

Are there patterns in your life that reveal a theme? If you have no sense of your purpose in life, do not worry. Most of us have no idea why we are here.

As a small child, I remember wondering and asking big questions. Even though my life was difficult at times, I had a vivid imagination. I was drawn to mystical stories and inspiring tales. I had some sense that my life had a purpose, but my purpose did not become clear until I was in my fifties.

After many years of spiritual seeking I have come to a conclusion: **I feel that we were all born with an inspired purpose. Some call it our soul purpose.** In this chapter, I invite you to explore deep within yourself and see what inspires you. We will look at how your values relate to your inspired purpose. We will also look at what might be holding you back from stepping into your inspired purpose. As we use several techniques to delve into this exploration, we might discover places where we need to love ourselves more, or we might reveal more superpowers. It's all expected along thc path to unveiling our inspired purpose.

As you think about your inspired purpose, or your "reason for being" so to speak, how does it line up with your current career? For many of us, our career is based on needs or desires that are driven by unconscious beliefs and patterns. You may be a doctor because that was what your parents told you to become. Or you squashed your desire to be an artist because you were led to believe you would always be poor. So, you got an MBA instead. Many of these decisions bring financial success, but they rarely leave us feeling satisfied, let alone inspired.

Take a few minutes to recall if you had any sense of purpose as you were growing up.

Begin with Leading Questions

A great way to clear the path to discover your inspired purpose is to ask yourself leading questions. Before you begin, I invite you to pave the way with the following affirmation. Say it out loud a few times before beginning to answer the questions. I know it may feel silly; just do it anyway. Your brain will hear it and try to make you right.

"I see evidence of my inspired purpose everywhere I look."

There are so many people whose talents I admire. I remember dreaming of being a professional ice skater. Years late, I wanted to be an architect. For many reasons, I ended up on a different path. And my inspired purpose is still being revealed to me.

Our inspired purpose often overlaps with what we enjoy, what we are good at doing, and what the world needs. To help get clarity on your inspired purpose, ask yourself the following three questions:

- What do I love doing?
- What am I really good at doing?
- What do I do well that could make the world a better place?

Write down some ideas that come to mind:

If your inspired purpose still eludes you, here are some more questions to ponder:

- As a child, what brought me joy? Did I ever say, "When I grow up, I want to be a..."?

- What types of books or entertainment do I enjoy most? What are the topics of my favorite books or movies?

- What do I love to do, despite the fact that everyone thinks I am crazy?

- If I were diagnosed with a terminal illness and could only accomplish one goal, what would that goal be?

- What upsets me the most about what I see going on around the world?

- What do I keep doing even though it is sometimes unpleasant and often very challenging?

Imagine How You Will Be Remembered

The mass of men lead lives of quiet desperation, and go to the grave with the song still in them."
- Henry David Thoreau

One concept that really motivates me is the knowledge that I was given this precious life on this beautiful planet. I know I have gifts and talents that can make a positive difference in the world. If I squander my gifts and talents and do not fulfill my inspired purpose, I will be held accountable. I am not exactly sure what that means, but it motivates me nonetheless.

A great trick that can help you unveil your inspired purpose is to imagine how you would like to be celebrated. I invite you to write a toast that you would hope someone might offer at your 80th birthday party. Think of accomplishments for which you want to be remembered. These are clues to your inspired purpose.

A little twist on this exercise is to write your own obituary. It may feel morbid, but perhaps it is an easier exercise since, in your imagination, you don't have to worry about your ego getting carried away.

This entire exercise may seem awkward. Remember, you do not have to share it with anyone. If you have resistance to doing this exercise, perhaps you feel undeserving? You might want to go back to Step 1: Love All of Yourself.

As you work through these exercises, be patient with yourself. I have been working on clarifying my inspired purpose for the last 20 years. These exercises are guideposts. Think of this process as an exploration. Stay curious and have fun.

Create Your Personal Values Statement

The basis for revealing and living your life of inspired purpose is to deeply know yourself. This starts with knowing your own personal values.

Your personal values are foundational to who you are. They drive most of your life decisions and actions. Exploring and naming your personal values is a powerful step in creating your life of inspired purpose.

To begin, take a deep breath and empty your mind of any preconceived ideas. Let go of what you think you value. This will help you access your intuition.

Without a lot of thought, start listing personal values that come into your mind. Write quickly and list as many as you can until you run out of ideas.

If you feel stuck, think about what you admire in other people. Are they qualities you value in yourself? Think about judgments you have of other people. What are they doing that you dislike? Are they acting with prejudice? If that upsets you, then you might value tolerance of differences in others. If you judge someone harshly for lying, then you might value honesty.

Another way to tap your core values is to think about what you need to thrive. Do you value learning? Do you need to be surrounded by or spend time in nature? I personally have to have lots of trees in my life because they seem to feed my spirit.

Do you value good health? Maybe you value clean food and water, or freedom of choice.

Here are some possible values to stimulate your thinking: authenticity, achievement, adventure, authority, autonomy, balance, beauty, compassion, challenge, community, connection, courage, creativity, credibility, curiosity, fairness, fun, happiness, honesty, humor, influence, inner calm, justice, kindness, knowledge, leadership, learning, love, loyalty, meaningful work, notoriety, optimism, peace, personal growth, pleasure, power, recognition, religion, respect, responsibility, security, service, spirituality, stability, success, tenacity, trustworthiness, vulnerability, wealth, wisdom.

Take a few minutes and create a list of your personal values:

Next, look at your list and see if you can group similar values. Values like honestly, integrity, and accountability can go together. Compassion, caring for others, and sensitivity can go together under Love or Caring or some other group name that resonates with you. Once you are down to 8-10 groups, rank them in order of importance. This may be difficult, but know that you can keep all that are important to you.

As you finalize your list, imagine how it feels to live your values. Do you feel a sense of relief that you can move into the world while being true to yourself?

Are there values to which you aspire that you do not feel you are living at the moment? Think of ways you can align your actions more closely with your values. Share your desires with close friends and ask them to hold you accountable.

Your list is always fluid. You can continue to refine your values as you grow into your greatest self and live your life of inspired purpose.

Create Your Inspired Life Plan

To support you in pursuing your life of inspired purpose, consider your current living situation and what will need to change to support you in reaching your goal. As you look at your current living situation, you can see what is missing for your life to support you.

Next, create a plan for your ideal life. Be very specific. Describe in great detail how you want it to flow and how you want to feel.

This exercise can sometimes activate a selfish behavior in us. So remember that you are showing up with your gifts for the greater good. While you want to be comfortable, you will not be happy if your plan focuses on material possessions.

For example, I enjoy being near nature, so I will make that part of my inspired life plan. I won't see myself having several vehicles or a huge mansion.

List the characteristics of your inspired life:

- What do you do each day?
- Where do you live? Describe your surroundings.
- Where do you work?
- How much income do you have? What type of income?
- Do you have a partner or partners?

Gap Analysis

What is not true today? Think about steps you can take to enable you to live your inspired life? This can be any number of things such as: more training, connecting with others, emotional clearing work, etc. Take action steps if they feel inspired. Otherwise, don't be attached to how everything unfolds. Think of it as "A shopping list for your angels."

Spend a little time each day reviewing your inspired life plan. Does it elicit positive emotions? Stay in the positive emotion for 15-20 seconds. This will help the universe bring you what you need for your highest good.

Share your plan with others or work in a group. You can get great ideas for ways to enhance and refine your plan.

Expand Your Mind - Visualize Your Life Without Limits

> *"You have sole ownership of your vision. And the Universe will give you what you want within your vision. What happens with most people is that they muddy their vision with "reality". Their vision becomes full of not only what they want but what everybody else thinks about what they want, too. Your work is to clarify and purify your vision so that the vibration that you are offering can then be answered."* - Esther Hicks (*Abraham and Jerry*)

Before we get down to the important work of unveiling and declaring your inspired purpose, you might want to see if you need to clear any blocking beliefs or traumas that are preventing you from resonating with your inner wisdom. Visualizing your life without limits is a great way to resonate with and attract what you need to reach your goals. Let's look at a few key areas and visualize what is possible.

Scarcity vs. Abundance

Many of us have an unconscious limit to our worth. Because of these unconscious beliefs, we limit our flow of abundance. Clearing our issues around self-worth and prosperity (in financial terms) is often quite effective in freeing us to feel more aligned with our inspired purpose.

Imagine you are given 50 million dollars without any restrictions. Ask yourself the following questions:

- What is the first thing I would do?
- How would my life be different?
- How would I spend the next week, month, and year?
- How could this support me in stepping into my inspired purpose?

Failure vs. Success

Fear of failure may be programmed into us at a very early age. If our parents lived with a lot of fear, this fear may be deeply ingrained in us.

When we imagine failing at something, we often catastrophize the consequences. Unveiling and clearing our fear of failure can unleash our power and inspiration. Ask yourself the following questions:

- What would I do right now if I knew I could not fail?
- What activities do I consider a waste of time to pursue?
- If I try something that scares me, what is the very worst thing that can happen?
- Will I have regrets 10 years from now, if I don't pursue my dreams? Will I be sorry if I always play it safe?

Fear of Success may be another fear that is programmed into us from a very early age. We may have been compared to others or shamed for being too smart, attractive or talented. This is very common for young girls who are raised in a male-dominated culture in which women are expected to be less smart and less capable than men. Ask yourself the following questions:

- What do I dare not do because people might say I am self-centered or showing off?
- What is the worst thing that could happen to me if I express myself to my fullest potential?

Create Your Inspired Purpose Statement

If you have no clue about your inspired purpose, try this little exercise. Read your list of superpowers to yourself. While you are reading your list, notice if your body is energized or excited by one or two of your superpowers. Imagine yourself in a situation where you are able to express it fully.

Do not be shy. In fact, be as grandiose as you can possibly be. No one is judging you, except possibly your inner critic. But remember, you can always tone it down afterwards. If you expand into your greatest inspired purpose imaginable, you are more likely to move beyond unconscious limitations.

Also, it is possible that you resonate with your inspired purpose because you feel it is what you came here to do. You may not realize any significant results in your lifetime. You are stepping into your inspired purpose to be of service to the greater good, so you don't want to be attached to any specific outcome or outcomes.

If you have a sense of your inspired purpose, start writing! If you don't have a clue, ask yourself the following questions:

- Whom do I admire?
- Why do admire them? What are they up to in the world?
- Would I like to participate in similar activities? If 'Yes', why?

Franklin Covey has a great tool for helping you develop your own mission statement, which is another way of expressing your inspired purpose. Check Resources in the Appendix for access to this tool.

Reveal Your Inspired Purpose

Another way to get to our inspired purpose is through the process of elimination. You will need a 3-inch square sticky note pad, a marker, and a whiteboard or blank wall area.

Think of five or more ideas about which you are passionate. Write each idea on a separate sticky note and put it on the whiteboard or wall.

Once you are done, stand back and take a few minutes to look them over. Then read them out loud.

Next, arrange them in order of importance to you. Put the idea that you are most passionate about at the top and then put each one below that in decreasing importance.

Now comes the hard part. One at a time, remove the bottom sticky note. If that is challenging, see if you can remove another one. Remember that this is just an exercise in priorities. It doesn't mean that you do not care about the other ideas. It is merely forcing you to prioritize so you can focus your time and energy on what is most important to you.

Repeat the process until you get down to a single sticky note. This can be very challenging. If you are really stuck, leave it for a day and come back. You can also ask yourself, "If knew I was going to die in a year and could only accomplish one thing, what would it be?"

When I first did this exercise back in 2003, I discovered that I have a desire to work within the prison system. I think this stemmed from research that showed how a majority of prisoners were abused before the age of 3. Today, I still feel drawn to work in the prison system. I can't imagine a place more in need of self-love.

Do not feel pressured to complete this in a single day. Spend a few weeks thinking about your activities, and spend an equal amount of time or more eliminating the ones that you must remove to get to that core activity, which may be your inspired purpose.

Ask for the Universe for Help

Have you ever had one of those experiences where you have a question and the answer is revealed through a sign or a dream? These are some of the ways to access our intuition or deeper wisdom.

Over the years, I've heard several stories about people who, while walking through a bookstore, had a book literally fell off the shelf into their hands that changed their lives. Others have expressed very clear guidance through dreams.

My personal favorite is to ask the universe to give me a sign. I give clear instructions that I need some answer or validation. I'll say, "I need a sign about X. And I want the sign to be so clear that I have no doubt it is the answer to my question. "

Early last year, I decided I wanted to move to another place in my local area. So I had started looking at houses. I was asking the universe for a sign to help me decide where to move. Then one evening I was reading a book that talked about a valley with trees near Los Angeles. As I read the words, I knew I had to move there. I started feeling real excitement about this adventure. Within six months, I was in my new location.

Another favorite is asking for guidance through my dreams. Before I go to bed, I say, "Spirit, please let me know anything I need to be of service for the highest good." I often wake up with ideas for an article or a new book. Or I'll hear a name of someone whose knowledge I want to pursue.

If you want more clarity about your inspired purpose, try some of these techniques. Or walk through a bookstore and see what grabs your attention. There are so many ways to get information. We just need to ask.

Ground and Seed the Vision of Your Inspired Purpose

Once you have an idea of your inspired purpose, there are many powerful ways to ground and seed it. In "The Awakened Women," Tererai Trent shares how her mother instructed her to follow their cultural tradition. She writes, "I buried my dreams under a rock as a reminder of the power of the earth and its connection to my umbilical cord, and of the power of a spiritual connection to something bigger than myself."[8]

Think of your inspired purpose as a treasure. A slight variation on Tererai's practice is write your inspired purpose or anything you want to manifest and hide it in a special place, like a beautiful box or jar. This sends a message to the universe that you want support.

Final Thoughts

Are you still not sure of your inspired purpose? Take heart. If you have the desire to know, it will be revealed over time. You may feel you are sure of your inspired purpose and then see it go through some variations. I suggest that you keep inquiring and noticing. Repeat the practices and ask for feedback from others.

Engaging with your tribe can help you unveil your inspired purpose. In Step 4: Engage with Your Tribe, I invite you to create structure in support of your inspired purpose to allow you to share your gifts or superpowers with the world. We all need to be sharing our gifts at this point in history.

STEP 4: ENGAGE WITH YOUR TRIBE

"We are not held back by the love we didn't receive in the past, but by the love we're not extending in the present."
- Marianne Williamson

Engaging with your tribe is an act of love. To connect deeply with others, we must be vulnerable. This requires trust. The degree to which we can be vulnerable is equal to the level of trust we have in our loved ones, our teams, our communities, and ourselves. As we step forward to give our gifts, we are stepping into a higher vibration or frequency – the trust frequency.

The Trust Frequency

"Personal transformation can and does have global effects.
As we go, so goes the world, for the world is us.
The revolution that will save the world is ultimately a personal one."
-Marianne Williamson

As you make a commitment to engage with your tribe, you are stepping into a frequency of trust with others. This trust frequency tells us to trust the loving universe. When you live in the trust frequency, love permeates your work and your life. **The Trust Frequency expands your awareness and enables you to step into your inspired purpose with an open heart, knowing that everything in our lives happens for us, not to us.**

In their groundbreaking book, "THE TRUST FREQUENCY: *Ten Assumptions for a New Paradigm*", authors Andrew Cameron Bailey and Connie Baxter Marlow offer a handbook for higher consciousness. ***The Ten Assumptions*** are a unique synthesis of indigenous cosmology, quantum science, and Eastern and Western mysticism.

The authors describe The Trust Frequency as, "The vibratory realm where the soul's destiny awaits, with more abundance, joy, beauty and peace than we can imagine. Examine core beliefs that stand in the way of the evolutionary upward spiral to higher consciousness. Align with your own inner knowing. Discover that the laws that apply to YOU differ depending on your frequency. Learn about the role of free will and our ability to choose our frequency, and thereby our reality. Enter a conscious, loving Universe."[9]

They describe the 7 A's of Consciousness as our requests to the conscious, loving universe, which determine our frequency and thereby our reality.

"*With expanded* AWARENESS *and accurate* ASSUMPTIONS, *we choose our* ATTITUDE, *consciously direct our* ATTENTION, ALIGN *with our highest inner promptings, take committed* ACTION *and* ALLOW *the Loving Universe to manifest beyond our wildest dreams.*"

This powerful statement has become one of my favorite affirmations. I encourage you to use it as a guide to manifesting your wildest dreams and beyond.

And finally, Andrew and Connie offer a glimpse of what is possible and how The Trust Frequency inspires our journey.

The High Road to Happiness

"The choice to move into the Trust Frequency triggers a shift to an elevated state of Being, individually and collectively. Once we learn to access this state of peace, love, beauty and abundance, we find ourselves operating at a completely different vibratory rate, where the laws and rules are different. Wisdom, prosperity and enlightenment are the order of the day. We are happy. How do we get there? We shift our consciousness.

How do we do that? We change our minds. It's that simple. We update our fundamental assumptions about the nature of reality, act according to our inner knowing, and our world changes accordingly. It's an infinitely more beautiful Universe than we ever suspected. This book takes us there, right to the heart of it. Since we can choose our own reality, let us create a life of grace and ease, abundance, beauty and balance."

Thank you, Andrew and Connie! The sharing of your insights and wisdom are such a gift to us all.

Our Many Tribes

Our first tribe is usually our family. From birth until we start pre-school or enter daycare, our family gives us our earliest reflection of who we are. As we get a little older, we may find other tribes among our school or neighborhood friends. As adults we may be parts of many tribes through work, play, and community.

Often, our expression during our early years may be very similar to how we desire to express ourselves now. If we are raised in a relatively safe environment, we often express our truest self while we still have our sense of innocence. However, early traumatic experiences can be the most difficult to understand and heal.

As adults, we are likely to have time alone. Some of us have a strong desire or need for alone time. Others enjoy spending more time with people. Between parents, siblings, roommates, spouses, children, and coworkers, I lived with other people until I was widowed in 2001. Following my husband's death, I spent many years living alone. This was powerful for my healing journey. I knew I needed to be happy alone if I wanted to be happy in any relationship, especially one with a significant other. In some ways, we could think of our first tribe as ourselves.

Our Tribe of One

"Four out of five of the voices in my head say 'Go for it'"
- Unknown

Have you ever had the experience of competing voices in your head? We all have different aspects of our personality that at times may be in competition with each other. When we make a mistake or have a regret, we can be very hard on ourselves. I have struggled with negative thoughts and self-judgment for most of my life. It wasn't until I really stepped onto my own healing journey and learned to love all of myself that I felt any relief from harsh self-judgement.

In Step 1: Love All of Yourself, we talked about our witness, that voice in our head that we hope will guide us in the right direction. In this section, Amy Myers contributes a powerful perspective and shares thought-provoking practices designed to help us to be our own 'best friend.'

We are often more harsh towards ourselves than towards others. In society, we are polite to people, as that's what we are supposed to be. But then if we get close to the self-talk that is often in our heads, we hear so much of the "I am not enough" or "I messed up again" or "I just can't get this right", or other similar critical messages. Just imagine how it would be if you had a friend who was constantly barraging you with these types of messages. I'm guessing that you wouldn't want to hang out with that person that much.

I still remember my dad first telling me "You have to be your own best friend." It was not really until I turned 48 years old and began a journey to self-love and spiritual connection/liberation, that I now feel the powerful meaning of this and the absolute practicality of it.

Society would not work if we were as hard on others publicly as we are on ourselves in our own heads, with our tendency towards negative self-talk. Friendships and family relationships would be even more unpredictable than they already are.

So *what if we thought of ourselves as a best friend? What if we gave ourselves the same loving care we would a best friend? What if we asked ourselves "Would I say this to a friend?" if we find that we are criticizing or finding fault in ourselves once again. What if instead we said "What would I say to a friend if they were feeling down, feeling less than adequate, feeling like they messed up or constantly got it wrong?"*

What if we asked ourselves, "What can I do today to take myself out for a wonderful day of my favorite things? What if I treated myself to a day free of self-blame, of being hard on myself? What if I start to give myself hugs even if they are figurative? What if I do physically hug myself?"

When we are looking at any new situation, whether it is a new relationship, new job, new city to live in, or new organization to volunteer for, what if we kept our standards high? Can you imagine yourself saying to a friend, here is what I wish for you in this new relationship, new job, new city, or new organization? Probably so. You probably have congratulated others, celebrated others, taken the time to acknowledge others and send best wishes to others much more than you have to yourself. Can we give to ourselves these same wishes, and hold high expectations for what we deserve?

I call this Conditions of Satisfaction. Early on when I had the good fortune to be selected for a special leadership coaching program at my company built upon Accomplishment Coaching, I learned about this exercise that is quite powerful. It's really getting rigorous with what you want in any situation, making your expectations clear: what is a must have, what is negotiable, what is non-negotiable.

I always liked this framework for helping you assess what you really want and the good things we all deserve. I have had enough situations where I simply live with the situation; I simply accept something as good enough or I am afraid to expect or don't think I deserve what I really want. And yet, I may at the same moment be telling someone else to fully expect what they truly want, to indicate they are worth what they really want in life. I see others struggle with this same full embracing of ourselves, fully asking for and expecting all they deserve, understanding that just by being themselves they deserve the best conditions, they deserve to be more than satisfied.

Some of this may be that as human beings with many aspects to ourselves, we are afraid of our dark sides, the parts of ourselves that we are embarrassed by, feeling that those sides make us less than good. Some of this may be what many in the human potential movement talk about; we are uncomfortable and scared of our greatness and brilliance. As Marianne Williamson *writes:* "Our deepest fear *is not that we are inadequate.* Our deepest *fear is that we are powerful beyond measure. It is our light, not our darkness that most frightens us.* We ask *ourselves, who am I to be brilliant, gorgeous, talented, fabulous?* Actually, *who are you not to be? Your playing small does not serve the world.*" As Gay Hendricks, PhD, *writes,* "Each *of us has an inner thermostat setting that determines how much love, success, and creativity we allow ourselves to enjoy.* When *we exceed our inner thermostat setting, we will often do something to sabotage ourselves, causing us to drop back into the old, familiar zone where we feel secure.*"

So why not get in touch with what you truly want and deserve, and articulate what your must-haves are in any situation. If it feels uncomfortable to ask for so much, then approach it as though you are advising your best friend; you are encouraging them to ask for what they want the most, for what they think they deserve.

Think about a situation you are facing, in your personal or your work life. This could be a new opportunity in your organization and you aren't sure how you feel about it; this could be a long-time relationship with a co-worker that is not going so well. This could even be a possible move to another state or country you are considering.

In any potential situation where you have a choice to make, there will be pros and cons and it's important to make sure that the choice you make is what you genuinely want, not what you think others think you should want.

Identify the choice you believe others around you would want you to make. It can help to put on paper what others may expect, as this can help free your thinking of the expectations of others.

Then, get in touch with what is truly in your heart, and if it helps, consider it as though you are talking to yourself as though you are talking to a dear friend.

Consider what you must have in the situation to be 200 percent happy and satisfied.

Consider what you must NOT have or ask your best friend what she/he must NOT have in the situation to be 200 percent happy and satisfied.

Consider what you are negotiable on.

Our Tribe of Friends

Think of your closest friends. Where they are in their lives? What are their goals and dreams? Typically your closest friends will have similar values to your own. They might be great allies for you as you step into your inspired purpose. What follows is a group process that you can use to engage with your tribe of friends to support every member of your tribe.

Inspired Synch-Up™

Think about which of your friends are on a path towards their goals and dreams and might want support. Invite these friends to join you in a weekly or bi-weekly gathering designed to support each other in taking action towards your inspired purpose. Ideally, you will meet in person or by phone or web on a weekly basis to support each other.

A group of 3-4 people is ideal. Each meeting should follow a mutually agreed-upon process. The length of the meeting is usually less than one hour. Someone should keep track of time so each person gets a chance to share and get support.

The following process is a slight variation on the standard mastermind format. I find it works a little better for lifting my spirits and helping me feel the potential of my actions.

This process works best if you love and trust each other. Set an intention to listen with an open heart. Resist thinking about what you are going to say when someone else is talking. Trust that the perfect words will emerge when it is your turn to speak.

Here is a suggested format and sample dialogue:

- Begin with a short meditation – silent or guided
- Person #1 shares their intention or goal for the week (or other time period).
    - My goal is to write content for a new webinar.

Other members reflect back what they heard person #1 say. They may offer encouragement but should offer no suggestions or insights.
    - I am excited to hear that you are writing content for your new webinar.
- Person #1 shares if they are having any issues with writing their new webinar.
    - When I sit down to write, I can't seem to get my creative juices to flow.
- Each member takes a turn making suggestions
    - I find the best time to write is early in the morning before my left brain becomes too engaged.
    - Ask someone to ask you questions like, "If you were going to create a webinar, what would you include in it?" Make sure to record your answer.

I really encourage you to give this process a try. It can keep you focused on your path as you engage with your tribe of friends.

Our Corporate Tribe

Engaging with our corporate tribe can be very rewarding. What follows are some ways to engage on an individual level. Later in the chapter, we talk about some group activities that also build connection.

"Let us always meet each other with smile, for the smile is the beginning of love." Mother Theresa

If you are anything like me, you want meaningful connections in all areas of your life. I have worked in high-tech for the last 30 years.

It's full of people who 'think' for a living. And many are super smart. But they don't always use both sides of the brain.

In simple terms, scientists tell us that the left brain controls our linear thinking and the right brain controls our emotions. Since many of us work in positions that requires lots of linear thinking, we may lose access to our emotions.

Here are some simple strategies for using the emotional side of your brain for generating deep connections in the workplace.

- Be curious! Ask questions and listen carefully. Everyone wants to tell their story. At first, they might not seem like they want to share. In a corporate setting, many of us aren't used to people being interested in our personal lives. On the other hand, we all have stories to tell. And sharing stories can lead to deeper connection. So if you are with someone at work and want a deeper connection, ask them something like "How did you end up working in this field." Or "Did you always want to be a ***market analyst***?" (Substitute the appropriate title.) See their face light up as they begin to share their story.

- Smile. Just smiling at someone without any expectation can invite connection. It may take a little time. So be patient. If you consistently smile and look friendly, your coworkers will want to connect with you more deeply.

- If you are in a coworker's office or work area, notice if they have any pictures or interesting pieces of art. If they have photos of people who might be family members you might say, "What a nice photo. Is that your family?" If you notice a painting on the wall, you might say, "I love that painting! Is there a story behind it?" Again, most people love to share their story.

- If you make an effort to be friendly and some of your coworkers seem responsive, invite them to join you for lunch or coffee/tea. Going out for coffee or a meal allows the other person to experience connection outside the office where they may feel more relaxed.

- One of the least obvious but most powerful ways to connect deeply with others is to keep your own head and heart connected. Whenever you think of it, focus on your heart space. Imagine pink light flowing between your heart and head. The more you practice this, the more it becomes your natural state. This heart energy is felt by others as an attractive, welcoming sensation that will draw them towards you.

Caveat: There are some people who just don't want to connect. If you make an effort and fail, don't take it personally. If you come from your heart and do your best, you honor your own process while allowing others to have their chosen experience.
Think of someone with whom you would like to connect. What are some ways you can approach that person?

____

____

____

____

____

____

Our World Tribe

"Love all. Serve all." – Hardrock Café

You may be feeling ready to take your wisdom to a broader audience or tribe. This section offers some techniques for taking action.

Let's say you want to offer a workshop or plan an event or action that gives you an opportunity to express your inspired purpose. Share your idea with friends to get feedback and ideas. Invite them to help you with the planning and execution.

Tools of Engagement

Tricks and Tactics to Ignite Your Creative Flow

"We need not fear that we can lose anything by the progress of the soul. The soul may be trusted to the end." – Ralph Waldo Emerson "Love"

There are numerous tricks and tactics to help us accomplish our goals. Here are a few of my favorites.

Blockbuster

The Blockbuster is a tactic that you can use to create structure and accountability for yourself with the help of your tribe. Here is how it works.

Let's say you have a project that you need to finish. It might be a writing project, which is often the case for me. Perhaps you are preparing to deliver a presentation and you need to plan your talk and create slides, or maybe you just want to motivate yourself to do a mundane task like going through your emails or cleaning your desk. The Blockbuster tactic works for all of these. Here is the process:

1. Ask a friend or member of your tribe to be your accountability partner. It requires little to no time on their part. This is just a way to trick your brain into thinking that they are holding you accountable.

2. Decide on a time that you are going to start working on your task. Put it on your calendar. Block out an amount of time that is the minimum amount of time you want to commit.

3. Email your accountability partner and let them know that you have committed to working on your specific task from 10:00 AM to 11:00 AM, for example. NOTE: You may feel the urge to start before the designated time. You must wait until the time you stated. Once you start, you can go longer than the designated time as long as your creative juices are flowing.

4. After you complete the task, email your accountability partner and let them know. Share how it feels. Write something like, "I'm so happy I completed my task!" or "I'm proud of the fact that I did something I didn't want to do."

5. Celebrate! Treat yourself to something you enjoy like taking a walk or planning time for a relaxing bath or reading time, whatever feels like a nourishing treat as a reward for your efforts and accomplishments.

Take a few minutes and list out some mundane projects that might get done with the help of a Blockbuster.

Positive Aspects List

Imagine you have already reached your goals. How does that feel? Imagine you are fully living into your inspired purpose. How does that feel?

Your positive aspects list details all the wonderful things that will be true once you reach your goal. Creating a list of positive aspects can actually help you reach your goals. Here's how it works:

1. Sit quietly for a few minutes and imagine that you have accomplished your goal. If your goal is to fully live into your inspired purpose, imagine how that looks and feels.
2. Make a list of all the things you appreciate and all the ways you are celebrating, now that you have reached your goal.

When I set out to write this book, one of the first things I did was to create a list of positive aspects; a list of positive feelings that will result once this book is completed. Here is my list. I complete the sentence: Now that The LOVE@WORK Method™ is written...

1. I can schedule the day at the spa.
2. I am starting my next creative project.
3. I am celebrating my book completion with my family.

A list I am now writing is of positive aspects as I am living my inspired purpose. I am completing the sentence: As I live each day fulfilling my inspired purpose...

1. I am financially supported with ease.
2. I feel joy in everything I do.
3. I make a positive difference in the world.
4. My heart is open and my mind is strong.

I invite you to think of a goal or perhaps your inspired purpose and write a list of positive aspects as if you have completed your goal.

Fake it Until You Make It

If you are getting ready to share your wisdom in service to others, you may feel fear of just showing up in front of a group or camera. One trick I found that works is to fake it until you make it.

I used to think of a confident woman and pretend to be her. I noticed that when I pretended to be confident, people would respond to me as if I was confident. Eventually, I grew into being more confident.

You may feel resistant to stepping out and sharing your wisdom. I want to encourage you to find the courage. Your gifts and wisdom are needed in the world now more than ever.

Your Personal Action Plan

"Whatever you can do, or dream you can, begin it.
Boldness has genius, power, and magic in it!"
- Goethe

If you are anything like me, you resist structure. I love being spontaneous and going with the flow. Unfortunately, it does not always support me in getting things done. It is especially challenging for me if I want to reach a long-term goal.

The following process is a framework that helps you create a strategy towards your goals and take frequent actions to step into service that is aligned with your inspired purpose. You can do it for yourself. However, it is especially powerful when done with a partner or group, preferably someone from your tribe.

There are five sections within this process:

- Declare Self-Affirming Statement
- Create Long Term Goals
- Share Successes
- Request Assistance
- State Action Steps

Let's say you are partnering with a friend to work towards your goals. You decide to meet on a weekly basis to share your progress. Agree on a time limit and stick to it.
The night before you meet, write out your information for the five sections. Email your completed document to your partner.

When you actually meet, take turns sharing your progress. You can both go through the entire document each week, or you can take turns. Test different ways to share your progress. Just completing the sections each week helps keep you on track.

Declare Self-Affirming Statement

Write a statement that reflects your values and describes your ideal life as if it exists right now. Also state underlying tenets that affirm your fundamental understating of how the universe works. Think of it as an affirmatio of what you are creating by stating that it is already true. This self-affirming statement will not change on a weekly basis. But it is good to read it out loud each time you meet and review your document.

Since this statement represents the future vision, my self-affirming statement is as follows:

"*I affirm and experience that I am an integral part of a loving and abundant universe. I joyfully share my gifts with the world in service to the greater good. I enjoy ease, love, and abundance in every area of my life. The universe lovingly brings me opportunities to expand my awareness and refine my actions and attention. I am fully supported in living my inspired purpose.*"

I invite you to take a few minutes and write a positive statement that reflects how you see yourself in cocreation with the universe.

Create Long-Term Goals

Declaring your long-term goals is a powerful way to attract what you need to reach your goals. I suggest that you state one-year, three-year, and five-year goals. If you are young and want to go further, add a list of ten-year goals. Cover areas such as health, finances, lifestyle, career accomplishments, relationships, and even spiritual goals. Start with your ten-year goals and work your way backwards. Here are some examples:

1-Year Goals

- 10,000 Twitter followers
- 5,000 Facebook 'Likes' on professional page
- 5,000 YouTube subscribers
- Written and published 8 books
- 5 products developed
- Passive income of $XXX per year
- Work 6 hours a day, 4 days a week
- Working with a partner
- Healthy diet and pain free

3-Year Goals

- 50,000 Twitter followers
- 10,000 Facebook 'Likes' on professional page
- 10,000 YouTube subscribers
- Written and published 14 books
- 18 products developed
- Passive income of $XXX per year

- Work 5 hours a day, 3 days a week
- Working with a partner
- Healthy diet and pain free

5-Year Goals

- 100,000 Twitter followers
- 50,000 Facebook 'Likes' on professional page
- 50,000 YouTube subscribers
- Written and published 25 books
- 25 products developed
- Passive income of $XXX per year
- Work 2-3 hours a day, 3 days a week
- Working with a partner
- Healthy diet and pain free

Share Successes

This section can be a lot of fun. Many of us are trained to be humble and demure about our successes. Sometimes we are shamed for feeling good about our accomplishments. This does not serve anyone.

I encourage you to write several sentences that state what you accomplished over the past week, or since you last met with your partner. Literally brag about what you got done. I think of it as completing the following sentence:

I am grateful for accomplishing... (Or for fun)

I brag that...

- I published an article in a conscious business magazine.
- I booked a paid speaking event for February.
- I developed 3 new product ideas.
- I received a payment from one of my clients.

Showing appreciation for our accomplishments tells the universe that we are ready for more. If you are working with a partner, this is where your partner can share your joy and acknowledge you for your successes.
I invite you to take a few minutes and write down some successes you had in the last week. It may feel awkward at first. If you are not used to celebrating your successes, this will feel like a new muscle. It is a good exercise because it raises your vibration so the universe will bring you more.

Request Assistance

This is where we tap into the fact that we live in a loving, supportive universe. I like to think of it as asking my angels for help. If we ask, we often get what we need, or something better.

I leverage this aspect of the process quite heavily. I approach it by finishing the following sentence:

I intend and allow spirit to manage...

- Continue to guide me to my highest good.
- Supply structure, focus, and motivation to write each day.
- Help with balancing work and play.
- Improve my awareness of ideas for bringing my work into the world.
- Bring paid speaking opportunities.

I am always amazed at the power of this process. I invite you to write down a few tasks for which you would like help from the universe. A fun way to think about it is as a shopping list for your angels.

State Action Steps

State some tasks that you want to accomplish in the next one or two weeks. This can be part of a project. I often break big projects into little chunks, especially when I am working on a book. I approach this step by completing the following sentence:

I commit to accomplishing this week...

- *Clean desk and office area.*
- *Complete another chapter in book.*
- *Finish client analysis.*
- *Meditate each morning.*
- *Walk, stretch, eat well, and feel gratitude every day.*

I encourage you to review your plan every day. There is power in reminding yourself of your intentions and desires.

Your Corporate Action Plan

"In the age of complexity,
we all need to think of ourselves as leaders."
- Olivia Parr-Rud

We live in an exciting time! Technology is changing so fast that it is hard to stay current, and there seems to be no end in sight. On an organizational level, this rapid change presents serious challenges, as well as amazing opportunities. If you want your organization to thrive, you have to learn to think and act differently.

Take leadership. Clearly the old fear-based, top-down, command-and-control style of leadership just does not work anymore. By the time a market opportunity or threat is identified, goes up the ranks to the CEO for a decision, and comes back down, the opportunity is lost or the threat is real.

Today, we need to empower everyone in our organizations to sense changes and respond quickly at every level. In this environment, the role of the leader shifts from a high commander to a coach and cheerleader, who values and empowers his or her employees within a culture of trust and connection. Given the degree of technical competency needed at every level, I argue that we all need to think like leaders.

In my work as a data scientist, I am a consultant, so I do not have direct reports. However, I still have to think like leader to be effective. Why? Most of my stakeholders have no idea how I do my analysis. I have to take responsibility for delivering solutions that meet their goals. I have to connect with them and lead them to a level of understanding that allows them to trust my analysis and suggested solutions. I have to think about how the business is affected by implementing my solutions. Since they do not understand the complexity of my process, I need to think through all the business ramifications of anything I recommend.

As new models of leadership take hold in our organizations, methods and processes are emerging that help leaders at every level become more agile and resilient. As we delve into a few important development areas, think of how you might bring out your own leadership qualities.

Deep Connection Builds Trust

The next time you are in a room waiting for a meeting to start, look around. How many people are looking at their phones? As the meeting gets started, notice how many people still spend a majority of their time still looking at their phones. It is possible that people do not feel connected to their coworkers because it is not encouraged or modeled. It takes effort to be present to another person or group of people, and it takes some courage to be vulnerable.

We all have the ability to create deep connections with others. Take a minute and recall how you feel when someone shares something that feels deeply personal. Do you suddenly feel more trusting of that person?

____

____

____

____

____

____

____

____

GROUP EXERCISE #1: VULNERABILITY - The following exercise invites you to enhance your connection with your teammates or coworkers through deep sharing. Brené Brown states, "... vulnerability is the cradle of the emotions and experiences that we crave. Vulnerability is the birthplace of love, belonging, and joy."[10] Before beginning any group exercise, I encourage you to set ground rules. Let everyone know that what is said in the exercise is confidential. Ask participants to suspend judgement and listen with an open heart.

Invite each person to finish one or more of the following sentences. Notice that some are positive while others may be a little more negative.

"Something funny that you don't know about me is ________________
____."

"My favorite hobby outside of work is __________________________
____."

"As a kid, I loved to ____
____."

"As a kid, I hated to ____
____."

"As a kid, my parents were always telling me to __________________
____."

"As a kid, my parents were always telling me to stop________________
____."

"I still feel uncomfortable sometimes when I____________________
____."

"The thing I most enjoy doing that I have to do is________________
____."

"The thing I least enjoy doing that I have to do is________________
____."

"The one thing for which I am most grateful is____________________
____."

"The one thing I would like to eliminate in my life is______________
____."

I am sure you can think of many more. These can be fun and they can become very deep, depending on the group. Once the process is complete, invite participants to share what they thought of the process. Ask if anyone feels more comfortable with their teammates or group members.

Take a few minutes to write down a few of your personal thoughts and insights. Did you learn anything about your coworkers that surprised you?

____

____

____

____

____

____

____

____

____

GROUP EXERCISE #2: PLAY - Another powerful way to build trust is to play together. I invite you to plan a day or an evening away from the office where you can just have fun. I have been involved with teams that went bowling or played softball. Another team event I enjoyed was an evening in an Escape Room. The event was really fun with a group of analysts! Even a hike or a game night can be a great way to build connection and trust.

Following your group event, I invite you to meet and share how you enjoyed the event. Another option is to create an internal webpage where everyone in attendance is invited to share what they enjoyed about their experience.

There are many other ways to deepen the connections within our organizations. **Deep connection, based on trust, is essential for collaboration, problem solving, and innovation. Trust is foundational to the success of every other goal for your organization.**

Effective Communication Enhances Teamwork

When we talk about barriers to communication, a common example is the variety of languages that are spoken in many companies. Working in the technology field, I have had many coworkers whose first language was not English. I have studied a few foreign languages, but nothing that would serve me well in another country. So, when I am asked if I speak any language other than English, I jokingly say that I speak SAS. As an analyst, I have used SAS programming for 30 years. I realize that may sound silly, but it illustrates the point that many technical jobs use languages that do not fit the classic definition, and language affects how our brains are wired.

The way our brain is wired affects our thinking and communication style. I remember being in several companies where I would listen to conversations between the Marketing and IT departments. Many times it seemed like they were speaking two different languages. I would witness conversations where they literally could not understand each other. Their words were in English, but they did not share common goals or challenges.

The following simple exercises help to improve communication with your coworkers and team members.

GROUP EXERCISE #3: ACTIVE LISTENING - One of the main reasons for poor communication is our inability to listen. Other reasons range from an aggressive speaking style to the use of vague language. In this exercise, I invite you to engage in active

listening. The exercise takes place between two people. For training purposes, others can observe and provide feedback.
This exercise is a dialogue between two people, the person sharing (Sender) and the person listening (Receiver). It is especially powerful when discussing a difficult topic.

The exercise begins with the Sender and the Receiver sitting or standing and facing each other. The Sender begins by stating their issue. The role of the Receiver is to listen very carefully. Once the Sender is finished speaking, the Receiver says the following:

Receiver: "Thank you for sharing. If I heard you correctly, you said, "...(repeat what you heard them say)... Did I get everything correct?"

If the Sender says, "No," they then follow up by restating the issue. When complete, the Receiver restates the issue a second time. Then the Receiver asks again, "Did I get everything correct?"

If the Sender says, "Yes," then the Receiver asks if the Sender has anything to add or more to discuss. If the Sender says 'Yes," the process repeats.

Once the Sender is complete, the Receiver summarizes everything the Sender has conveyed. The Receiver might say, "Let me make sure I got everything you were saying," (followed by a recap).

Notice that the Receiver has not shared any opinions or suggestions. The role of the Receiver is to thoroughly understand what the Sender is saying. This is a great opportunity to practice being fully present to someone else. Giving someone your full attention is an act of generosity.

If you want to take this practice to a higher level, you can invite the Receiver to feel compassion for the Sender. The Receiver can say things like, "I sense that you are upset. Is that true?" If the Sender says, "Yes," the Receiver could respond with "Would you like to talk about it?"

These conversations can go quite deep. The key skill for both participants to practice is to stay present and share their thoughts in the moment without judgement.

Take a few minutes to write down some of your personal thoughts and insights.

GROUP EXERCISE #4: NONVERBAL COMMUNICAITON - Nonverbal communication is the process of sending and receiving information or messages without using words, excluding both spoken and written words. Research suggests that a majority of our communication is nonverbal. Most of us are familiar with the concept. However, many of us are not aware of the effect it has on ourselves and others.

There are seven types of nonverbal communication as defined by Judee Burgoon:[11]

1. Body movement, posture, and eye movement.
2. Voice inflection, volume, pitch, and timbre.
3. Personal appearance.
4. Physical environment, personal surroundings.
5. Personal space, closeness.
6. Touch.
7. Time, such as lateness, speed, etc.

As members of a group, I invite you to explore your own nonverbal communication styles with a variation on the game of charades. It can be quite fun and revealing. To start, pass out 2-3 strips of paper to each person. Everyone writes an emotion or attitude on their strips of paper. All the strips of paper are put into a bowl or other container.

One at a time, each participant pulls out a strip of paper and uses nonverbal communication to help the team guess their emotion or attitude. Once all the papers are used up, take time to debrief. See if you learned anything about yourself and your coworkers or team.

Take a few minutes to write down some of your personal thoughts and insights.

Rich Diversity Fuels Innovation

If you work in a sizable company, I am sure you experience rich diversity among your coworkers. The most obvious types of diversity are age, race, and gender. Less obvious types of diversity include education level, years of experience, religious affiliation, political affiliation, and more.

What I find fascinating is how people's styles and strengths vary greatly within an office setting. With advances in technology, we may want to rethink how we value these styles and strengths. Let me explain.

Years ago, most linear tasks like accounting and data management were done by hand. These skills required lots of left-brain talent. Today, most left-brain activities are being automated or outsourced. This is glaringly apparent with the introduction of Artificial Intelligence.

The result of this trend is that to be successful, we all have to use our whole brains. With automation leveling the playing field, we have to create and innovate to be successful. This means we have to take more risks, and we need to trust each other.

The following exercises are designed to tap into our creativity and leverage our diversity.

EXERCISE 5: BRAINWRITING – You are probably quite familiar with the concept of brainstorming. This can be a powerful and fun exercise to stimulate new ideas and 'out-of-the-box' solutions to problems through unfettered verbal exchange. However, brainstorming may not work for every group since it often ends up being dominated by a few individuals. Brainwriting is a simple variation that, like the previous exercise, honors everyone's ideas and styles.

The goal of the exercise is to come to up to one or more solutions for a single problem. It is important that the problem be stated very clearly.

This process works best at a conference table. You will need a stack of index cards and pens for everyone. Begin by clearly stating the problem or issue. Then each person quietly takes a card and writes a solution. Like brainstorming, you put everything you think of – no filtering and no self-judgment. Anything and everything goes.

Once you have written down your first solution, put it back into the center and grab another index card. If someone has already written a solution, see if you can enhance or tweak it.

Limit the first session to 20 minutes. Then take a short break and reconvene. If everyone feels like they want to continue, repeat the process for another 20 minutes.

When complete, each person reads a card until you have read every proposed solution. You will be amazed at what you discover. I worked with a large bank using this process. They wanted to come up with an original name for their data warehouse. I cannot share the particulars due to confidentiality, but I will say that the name they chose was a spectacular hit with the senior leadership team.

Take a few minutes to write down some of your personal thoughts and insights.

EXERCISE 6: COMMUNICATION STYLE – Diverse opinions and points of view are proven to fuel innovation and enhance organizational progress. In addition to the familiar types of diversity, a greatly underappreciated type of diversity is communication style.

In the previous exercise, I pointed out how brainstorming can end up being dominated by a few individuals with strong, outgoing personalities. Team members who are quieter by nature are better leveraged through brainwriting.

The process I am inviting you to employ is called Six Thinking Hats® by Edward de Bono.[12] It is also a powerful way to tap the wisdom of team members with more passive personalities.

Here is how it works: State a problem you would like to solve and a few suggested solutions. These solutions may have come from the prior brainwriting exercise.

The exercise magnifies our different personality styles. The six colors of hats represent different ways that people tend to behave when they are solving problems:

- White: Facts are often written on white paper. What are the facts (data and information) about the problem and suggested solution?
- Red: Emotions can create heat. How do you feel about the solution?
- Black: Danger. What are the difficulties or problems with this solution? What could go wrong?
- Yellow: Sunshine and optimism. What is great about this solution? What are all the positive aspects?

- Green: Sprouting new ideas. What are the alternatives to this approach?
- Blue: High in the sky overview. What is our next step? How do we proceed and integrate our solution?

Think about using this process when you have a decision that has to be made and you have reached a stalemate, or when the discussion is taking too long and you need to reach a decision quickly.
I invite you to try a few ways of using the Six Thinking Hats® process. Feel free to come up with your own variations. It is a very flexible process that can be adapted to suit your unique needs.

- One way to use the Six Thinking Hats® process is to invite the entire group to discuss the problem and solution using one color hat at a time. They might begin with the White hat. Going around the table, each person is asked to state the facts as they perceive them. By the end of the round, everyone should be clearer about the facts. Then the group moves to the Red hat and shares how they feel about the problem and solution. The process continues until every person has spoken from the perspective of each color hat. What you might notice is that some people are very comfortable with one or two styles but the other styles make them uncomfortable. For example, very left-brain engineers might not like to share how they feel. Other emotional types might have trouble just sticking to the facts. Negative people might find it challenging to be optimistic. It is a great way to stretch outside of our comfort zone.
- If you have a team that already works well together and want to get through the process a little faster, you can assign each person a hat color or let them select the color they want. Encourage team members to take a hat color that is not their

usual style of interaction. Continue the discussion until the group's time limit is reached or until everyone is satisfied. Also, allow people to switch hats within the same meeting. It can be really interesting to see how people interact when they are outside of their usual behavior style.

Note: You do not need literal hats. But, some groups have fun with actual hats of different colors. Typically, you have a visual handy for reference.

After your meeting, take a few minutes to write down some of your personal thoughts and insights.

Embracing Change Enables Agility

Our businesses are going to face new challenges whether we like it or not. We can either be surprised and reactive or we can be prepared and proactive. Early in my career, I always felt like my life was out of control. I lived with a lot of stress. As my work began to have a positive impact, I went through several mergers and acquisitions. At first, I found it terrifying. But after each transition, I landed on my feet and felt stronger. After 10 years of constant turmoil, I landed in a high position at a large bank. After a few months, I was overcome with dread. At that moment, I knew that my position, office, projects, and manager were not going to change in quite a while. I was actually getting bored, and I missed the stimulation of the unknown. That was when I decided to become a consultant. I never looked back.

Discomfort with change can show up in many ways. The following exercises explore some underlying, even unconscious reasons why we may be resisting change. If your organization is not dealing with any major changes at the moment, you can create an imaginary scenario for the sake of the exercise. For example, imagine a larger company is purchasing the organization.

Both of the following exercises are carried out in a group discussion. I recommend establishing ground rules. Before you begin, let the group know that only one person talks at a time. There is no cross talk, no suggestions, and no discussion. It may be helpful to have the speaker hold something like a pen or rock that signifies that it is their turn to speak. All participants are encouraged to deeply listen.

EXERCISE 7: ATTACHMENT - Go around the group and have each person answer the question, "What am I attached to that I think I can never give up?" Continue going around the room until everyone has participated or your reach your time limit. After you feel the exercise is complete, spend a few minutes discussing the process. Notice if you feel closer to the other participants.
Take a few minutes to write down some of your personal thoughts and insights.

EXERCISE 8: LOOKING FOWARD - Go around the group and ask each person to name one thing they are losing and one thing they are gaining in the upcoming transition. Keep going around until everyone is complete or you reach your time limit. After you feel the exercise is complete, spend a few minutes discussing the process. Notice if you feel closer to the other participants.

Take a few minutes to write down some of your personal thoughts and insights.

Final Thoughts

Are you getting excited about fully stepping into your inspired purpose and sharing your superpowers with the world? And are you ready to claim your position as a leader? Remember: the people in your life, whether they are members of your tribe or your teammates, want you to flourish. They want you to fully express yourself. By doing this, you inspire them to fully express themselves.

By using the tools in this chapter and beginning to engage with your tribe, you are stepping into your destiny. If you still feel stuck or afraid, go back to Step 1: Love All of Yourself. Review all the earlier chapters to remind yourself of your amazing superpowers. Remember your inspired purpose that the world needs you to share. Do not worry if you are not perfect. It is not about you. This is what evolution is asking of us: that we all show up fully in service to the greater good. Your actions will inspire others!

AS LOVE

"If you give your life as a wholehearted response to love, then love will wholeheartedly respond to you."
- Marianne Williamson

We are blessed to live in extraordinary times. Our consciousness is evolving. As energetic beings, we are shifting from a frequency of fear, to a frequency of love. I feel this is why so many of us are being called to share our gifts. The world needs our wisdom.

I invite you to think of this time as a new beginning. Now is the time to act on that desire to fully express yourself. Now is the time to use your gifts to make the world a better place. My hope is that by practicing the LOVE@WORK Method™ you feel more inspired and confident to take the next step towards expressing your inspired purpose and making a positive difference in the world.

Know that you are well on your way to healing your wounds, the life experiences that made you who you are today. You are getting ready to step into your greatness and share your wisdom, and live your life of inspired purpose. As you do, I hope this practice guide will become a favorite companion.

As you heal and bring forward your gifts, you are raising your vibration. You are learning to trust yourself. You are learning to trust your wisdom. You are increasingly holding a higher frequency – the frequency of love.

With that in mind, I would like to invite you to think of love a little differently. Rather than something you do, I want you to think of love as a way of being.

Being 'love' is about living in your heart. As you heal and learn to really love yourself, you can stand vulnerably with an open heart. You will feel love for everyone and everything.

Being 'love' may not feel natural at first. Initially, you may need to set an intention to drop into your heart throughout the day. You might be thinking, "I can't possibly do that. I often engage with people who are angry or unkind." In my experience, it is in challenging situations with very difficult people that this practice is most powerful. With enough practice, you will eventually feel love in everything you do.

Know that there are always bumps along the way. I regularly return to the self-love exercises. As we stretch and grow, we will keep bumping up against our wounds, our shadows, and our rough edges. These bumps are all part of the process, and it gets easier over time. Eventually, living 'as love' becomes effortless.

Think of yourself as a precious stone being honed and polished. The rough edges are disappearing. Your light is shining brighter and brighter every day. And the world needs your light!

ABOUT OLIVIA

Olivia is a global thought leader, data scientist, and award-winning and best-selling author. Her unique approach to business success draws on her passion for data science, holistic leadership, and human potential through a blending of left-brain and right-brain models and practices. Her latest research unveils the relationship between employee engagement, loving behavior (i.e. compassion, connection, and caring), and long-term corporate profits.

Olivia has a BA in Mathematics, an MS in Statistics, and is a lifelong learner with a passion for systems theory, quantum physics, psychology, and spirituality. Clients include Cisco, Walmart, Wells Fargo, Fleet Bank, HBSC, Genentech, State Farm, Nationwide, Liberty Mutual, Clorox, HP, IBM, SAS, and Xerox.

Engage with Olivia

Olivia works with individuals and groups who have the desire to take their growth to the next level and make a positive difference in the world. She specializes in working with people who want to bring their love and light into the corporate world through strength and vulnerability.

Olivia offers customized programs as well as individual and group coaching and webinars. Olivia is also available for speaking engagements and business consulting. Please visit ***www.oliviapr.com*** for a full list of offerings and the latest events and products.

What is Your Self Love Quotient?

Would you like to know your Self-Love IQ? Take the Self-Love IQ assessment at ***www.selflovequotient.com***.

What is Your Corporate Love Quotient?

Would you like to know your Corporate Love IQ! Take the Corporate Love IQ assessment at ***corporatelovequotient.com***.

Other Books and Contributions by Olivia

***Data Mining Cookbook, Modeling for Acquisition, Risk and Customer Relationship Management* (Wiley 2001).**

Written for data scientists, this highly technical book provides steps to build, validate, and implement statistical models using SAS® software. It is a global bestseller and is available in three languages.

***Business Intelligence Success Factors, Aligning for Success in a Global Economy* (Wiley/SAS, 2009).**

After spending years consulting for numerous companies in a variety of industries, Oliva saw the need to educate data-driven organizations on the value and power of their human capital. She spent years researching the financial and emotional benefits of effective communication, collaboration, and leadership in large organizations. This led to the unveiling of links between the global economy, organizational dynamics, and complexity science detailed in this groundbreaking book.

Business Analysis Using SAS® Enterprise Miner® and SAS® Enterprise Guide®, A Beginner's Guide

Awarded Best of Show at the Carolina Technical Book competition in 2014-2015, this book is written for data scientists who use SAS® software, this book details steps in building effective predictive models. Each chapter includes a section to help data scientists take their highly technical results and effectively translate them for their business stakeholders.

LOVE@WORK, *The Essential Guide to a Life of Inspired Purpose*

An international best-selling book that makes a compelling argument for bringing love into business. Using data and historic research, Olivia suggests that love, defined as compassion, caring and connection, are good for the bottom line as well as the employees, their families, their communities and the world at large. Olivia then introduces the LOVE@WORK Method™ to help us open our hearts and show up fully in service to the greater good.

Empowering YOU, Transforming Lives!: Daily Inspiration to Help YOU Live on Purpose and With Purpose

Olivia contributed to this powerful and heart-centered 365 daily inspiration book designed to encourage, uplift and empower you each and every day of the year. This inspirational and motivational book has been created by 40 authors coming together to lean into you on a daily basis, each of them encouraging you one day at a time to live on purpose and with great purpose.

Due out in October 2019

LOVE@WORK *for Business, Models and Methods for Building a Culture of Love*

Research shows that companies whose leaders create a culture of love, defined as compassion, caring, and connection, enjoy higher profits. LOVE@WORK for Business will dive into the models and methods used by organizations that allow for a culture of love to emerge.

Email Address: contact@oliviapr.com
Phone Number: 215 948-3500
Website: ***www.LoveMakeItYourBusiness.com***
Facebook page(s):
https://www.facebook.com/LoveMakeItYourBusiness/
LinkedIn Page: ***https://www.linkedin.com/in/oliviagroup/***
Twitter handle: OliviaParrRud
Instagram: parrrud
YouTube: ***www.OliviaOnYouTube.com***
Radio Show ***www.quantumbusinessinsights.com***
Other Social Media Channels: None
A portion of the profits go to The Oracle Institute.
www.theoracleinstitute.org

APPENDIX

Feedback
360° Feedback https://www.hr-survey.com/360Feedback.htm

Applied Kinesiology
http://www.holistichealthtools.com/muscle.html

Breathwork
https://www.goodtherapy.org/learn-about-therapy/types/breathwork

Energy Therapies
CLEAR® https://www.changeworksinc.com/what-is-clear/

Self-Care Assessment
https://socialwork.buffalo.edu/content/dam/socialwork/home/self-care-kit/self-care-assessment.pdf

Personal Mission Statement by Covey
https://msb.franklincovey.com/

The Trust Frequency
Connie Baxter Marlow
Andrew Cameron Bailey
www.TheTrustFrequency.net
www.First50Years.us

www.InSearchoftheFutureMovie.com
www.SacredEarthEnterprises.us

CONTRIBUTORS

Connie and Andrew

"In her ground-breaking book *LOVE@ WORK*, Olivia steps out to show how activating Love in corporate culture brings forth a soaring bottom line and makes businesses resilient and flexible in rapidly changing times. Olivia sees beyond the status quo/current reality into a new vibratory level where the unique gift of each individual is required for the symphony of life to resonate at its fullest magnificence. Her inspiring *LOVE@WORK METHOD*™ brings practical tools for accessing the personal self-love and inspired purpose necessary for global and business transformation." - Connie Baxter Marlow and Andrew Cameron Bailey, The Trust Frequency.

Connie Baxter Marlow is an author, filmmaker, photographer and futurist. Her uplifting worldview offers practical means of transcending the current paradigm through absolute trust in a conscious loving abundant Universe. She has co-authored the book **"THE TRUST FREQUENCY: *Ten Assumptions for a New Paradigm*"** which synthesizes indigenous cosmology, quantum science and Eastern and Western mysticism into a framework that resolves several paradoxes which have plagued humanity for millennia and have kept us from walking in alignment with the love we carry in our hearts. She pro-actively seeks to bridge the gap of separation between indigenous and non-Indigenous worldviews through films, books, forums and inter-cultural relationships. She and her partner Andrew Cameron Bailey have spent decades with their First Fifty Years Project, bringing forth the perspective that inter-cultural syntheses occurred between the European colonists and the American Indian which gave birth to the American mind, spirit and democracy. She believes the only way out is UP to higher consciousness. She is producer of the films **"IN SEARCH OF THEFUTURE: *What do the Wise Ones Know?*"** and **"SEEDS OF FREEDOM: *A Vision forAmerica*"**.

Andrew Cameron Bailey, filmmaker/photographer/inventor/author is a visionary thinker in the realms of climate change mitigation and the evolutionary potential of humanity. He has degrees in anthropology, chemistry and chemical engineering, and has lectured in organic chemistry and mathematics at the college level. He is the founder of Circular City Consulting, LLC, and is developing economically-viable climate change solutions. He is co-author of "The Trust Frequency: Ten Assumptions for a New Paradigm," author of the historical mystery novel "The Mayflower Revelations" and director of the films "**IN SEARCH OF THE FUTURE: *What do the Wise Ones Know?*"** and **"SEEDS OF FREEDOM: *A Vision for America*"**.

www.TheTrustFrequency.net
www.First50Years.us
www.InSearchofTheFutureMovie.com
www.SacredEarthEnterprises.us

Amy Myers

Amy Myers is a self-love practitioner and healer. On a journey to fully appreciate herself since she was born, she healed herself of chronic pain and a possible life in a wheel chair once she fully embraced all sides of herself and the dark and light in this world.

On a daily basis, she serves the world through her business Possibilities Connected where she helps clients transform their visions into reality. With a special emphasis of bringing more connection, appreciation and celebration into the work world, she dreams of a day when the world is focused on all that is going well, celebrating every iota of goodness all around us, soaking up the beauty of everyday daily life and the genius that is manifest in all of us and using that energy to tackle the world's greatest challenges.

With a personal passion for integrated problem-solving, 20+ years corporate experience in transformational roles including 16+ years in global leadership roles, and expertise in change leadership, group and team dynamics, strategy development and deployment, Amy is known by those she serves as a partner who helps clients achieve far more than they ever thought possible in a manner that brings out the best in people through a process that is truly enjoyable and enriching. Her clients highlight that whatever she works on with them ends up sticking in their organizational and team cultures and delivers real business impact.

Ultimately, Amy is passionate about doing all she can in the world to help others fully appreciate and love ourselves, as she believes that this will naturally lead to the appreciation and love for others, with the power and energy to elevate humanity to a more peaceful, harmonious and abundant world.

https://www.linkedin.com/in/amymyerschicago/

Thanks,
Amy

Amy Myers Principal
+1.312.593.6987
amy@possconn.com

Bethany Rivett-Carnac

Bethany is the Founder of Love Led Coaching Ltd, where she creates spaces for trailblazers led by a divine desire to make a positive difference in the world to sink into their intuition, honour their heart's calling and recognise what they are being led to create next in their world. She believes that creating the right space for creativity and individuals to bloom is essential and the spaces she invites clients to play in and co-create are inspired by the beauty of nature, the sacredness of ritual, the power of presence and engaging the senses, the sanctity of energy and the comfort of cosy.

She hosts retreats, workshops, one to one sessions and women's circles, along with webinars and online gatherings. All centred around opening up to inspiration, creating the fertile ground for us to bloom and each person owning, celebrating and wholeheartedly expressing their own journey and their gifts. One of her favourite mantras in life is, 'You be you, I'll be me and together, let's be us'.

Bethany was led to this work during her love LED fertility journey, which saw her making large shifts in both her personal and professional life; recognising where her creativity needed more room to grow, what was stifling her blooming and uncovering gifts and tools to help her find fulfilment in life. She now holds the space for other women going through their own fertility journey through in person and online 'Sacred Fertility' circles and one to one coaching and healing sessions.

Prior to love LED, Bethany's work always centred around people, through work in HR, Talent Acquisition, Learning and Development and Collaboration. Since opening up to her own creativity, she also has experience in Graphic Facilitation and Illustration. She has worked for a variety of organisations from a small family run agency, through to an SME entrepreneurial educational expedition company for young people and a large, global manufacturing company.

www.loveledcoaching.co.uk

REVIEWS

David Dibble

"Finally! A book that proves to even the biggest skeptics that love, as the cornerstone of organizational culture, is simply good business. More importantly, Olivia gives us a roadmap for successfully bringing more love into our businesses as the methodology to significantly improve profitability and overall performance of the business. For business leaders and managers who want to improve both culture and the bottom line, read this book! You'll be glad you did."

David Dibble - Author, ***The New Agreements For Leaders*** and creator of the 7 Tools for Organization Change

linkedin.com/in/davidbdibble
https://www.facebook.com/David.B.Dibble
plus.google.com/109080646327542972930
youtube.com/channel/UChuBUvkWmPTQ0oWvGqK6Lww
twitter.com/david_dibble
https://thenewagreements.com/

Kathy Mason

"If you yearn for more meaning in your life, you should read and USE The LOVE@WORK Method™. Olivia has collected the most powerful and effective processes to have you shift your life from stress to joy quickly. It's a powerful, but easy to use, resource that I will use over and over again for clarity. I highly recommend it!"
Kathy Mason, Author and President, Mason Works

Kathy@masonworksmarketing.com
www.masonworksmarketing.com
https://www.linkedin.com/in/kathymason1/
https://www.facebook.com/profile.php?id=100016089224025
https://www.facebook.com/KathyMasonMarketing/
https://twitter.com/Kathy_Mason

Cell : 720-938-2536

Laura George

"The Love@Work Method – the companion workbook to Love@Work: The Essential Guide to a Life of Inspired Purpose – is a superb tool for self-evaluation and springboard for self-realization. In a skillful yet gentle manner, Olivia assists the reader in locating false identities, uncovering shadow elements, and identifying blockages that keep us from achieving inner peace. She then lovingly guides the reader to discover healthy self-love, their "superpowers," and their true life purpose. Over the years, I have read many inspirational books – including histories and disciplines of many masters and mystics – and I highly recommend this workbook as a holistic method for achieving self-inquiry and seeking self-actualization."

~ Rev. Laura M. George, J.D., Executive Director of The Oracle Institute and Oracle Institute Press, founder of the Valley of Light Community, and award-winning author of ***The Truth: About the Five Primary Religions***, ***The Love: Of the Fifth Spiritual Paradigm, and The Light: And the New Human***

Mike Jay

Thanks for the opportunity to say something about your book. One only need review the essence of the 4 steps to come into an "energy and information" necessary for our evolution as a living system. What's clear to my mind is that the weaving and braiding necessary for our own developmental journey is only enhanced through the application of the 4 steps into our own unique perspective. I couldn't recommend the book and it's 4 steps enough for those who are exploring the world as it is, and it could be.

Mike R. Jay, 2019
Developmentalist

https://leadu.com/buy-the-book-at-f-l-o-w/ and/or
https://leadu.com/inner-circle-membership/

Sue Brightman

My research of 100 about women over age 50 reveals the life-giving importance of so many things Olivia encourages in this workbook: being led by Love in one's life, using intuition and diligence to find purpose, connecting to a trusted tribe, and making sure we care for ourselves as much as we care for others. Parr-Rud's workbook is her offering to help us do these things, step by step. Bravo Olivia — and all of us who are on the path of continued learning and becoming."

~ Sue Marchner Brightman
Founder, Brightman Glover International Coaching and Consulting in Conscious Business

President, For Women on the Journey of Their Lives

Author, forthcoming ***Manifesta of Active Wisdom from 100 Women Over 50: A Call To Further Becoming***

Linda Patten

Learn the 'why' AND 'how' of purposeful leadership!

As a leader, when I have my team write out their 'why,' their first attempt tends to be rough and not very inspiring. Now I can use the Love@Work Method, a four-step, practical process to help us turn that first statement into a detailed vision that will move us into taking on the challenges of today. Using her own journey to a life of inspired purpose as a foundation for the steps in this workbook, Olivia Parr-Rud offers the 'why' as well as the how' for up-and-coming leaders to inspire leadership and meaningful change in today's world.

~ Linda F. Patten, Leadership Trainer for Women Entrepreneurs and Changemakers – President &CEO, Dare2Lead With Linda, Website: ***www.dare2leadwithlinda.com***, email: ***linda@dare2leadwithlinda.com***

www.dare2leadwithlinda.com
https://www.facebook.com/dare2leadwithlinda
https://www.facebook.com/linda.patten.311
https://twitter.com/patten_linda
https://www.linkedin.com/in/lindapattenhttp://www.youtube.com/c/LindaPatten
https://plus.google.com/+LindaPatten
https://www.pinterest.com/lindapatten311/

Marlene Elizabeth

Is your work environment driven by fear or love? Can love in the workplace increase profits? Are there financial benefits directly related to love-leadership? Olivia Parr-Rud's exciting book LOVE@WORK provides inspiring answers and intriguing data which powerfully supports her message that "love is the greatest driver of success in business today. " Olivia brilliantly leads readers on a captivating journey inside "companies rooted in trust, caring and authenticity". You'll also learn how to uncover your inspired purpose, powerful secrets to success, excellent tips for creating an inspired life plan, plus strategies for healing trauma and negative patterns. Love this book!!

- Marlene Elizabeth
Certified Money Coach®
and Bestselling Author of MONEYWINGS™

Website: ***www.GrowMoneywings.com***
Email: ***Marlene@MarleneElizabeth.com***
Facebook: ***https://www.facebook.com/growmoneywings/***

Julie Roberts

"Olivia Rud understands the power of love in business. In her book, LOVE@WORK she discusses processes for businesses to increase love in the workplace. This is incredibly important given our current discordant environment. People are the most important resource and when the work environment is loving people produce more. It is also critical for anyone who wants to reach their highest potential to remove unhealthy patterns (usually created by trauma and blocking beliefs). When we clear our old patterns, we can produce from a place of compassion and manifest a destiny we desire. Doing this requires time and commitment to clear the old and ongoing practice of stepping into the emotions and behaviors of who we want to be. Olivia leads us through this process."

Julie Roberts, Ph.D.
Change Works
610 329-6483

julie@changeworksinc.com
www.changeworksinc.com

Julie Ann

"Olivia has created a beautiful and practical pathway to help you tap into your purpose and bring your much needed gifts into the world. Step by step she leads you into a journey of self-discovery and empowerment. You just need to open the book and begin"
... Julie Ann, Author and Spiritual Coach at **JulieAnn.co**

Julie Ann is an Author, Intuitive Healer, Spiritual Mentor and Teacher. She is also the creator of

www.julieann.co
www.intu.com.sg
www.facebook.com/lookingforasign
www.facebook.com/seeing1111

Janet Straightarrow

"I met Olivia Parr-Rud at an Edgewalker Retreat in 2009, and was inspired by her passion to bring awareness and spirit to the work place. Her personal work and her commitment to sharing her wisdom learned and earned is powerful and needed in these times. The LOVE@WORK Method™ offers a concise and comprehensive workbook for people to begin and to continue to deepen their personal healing, awareness, team building, and leadership skills and journey. Olivia offers a complete set of processes and practices to get directly to the point in how to move forward personally and professionally. Self-Love is at the core of everything in our lives and Olivia offers ways to accomplish this. Bringing forward our higher self and purpose and how to accomplish it each day brings us into self-mastery at home, work or play. Brilliant. May this work awaken and support many.

"Janet StraightArrow of Be The Medicine, Is Healing, Wisdom, and Grace."

Be inspired daily on her Facebook page below and follow her on these links.
www.Facebook.com/janet.straightarrow
join her many pages and groups here.

www.twitter.com/Bethemedicine
www.Linkedin.com/janetstraightarrow
www.Instagram.com/bethemedicinenow
www.bethemedicine.com
Call 973-647-2500
Email **Janet@Bethemedicine.com**

Nancy Mills

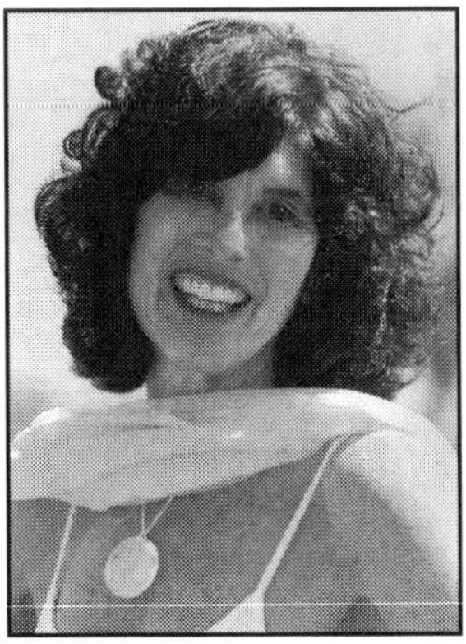

"It is not often that we meet an author who is on the pulse of what is needed, Olivia Parr-Rud, has written a book that is timely and will help many people."

Nancy Mills, The Spirited Woman (***www.thespiritedwoman.com***)

Jeanne Alford

Ever wanted a mentor that could help you improve yourself, your behavior or simply to bounce off ways to improve your outlook? In Olivia's companion workbook, you get just that. A step by step guide to integrate all the lessons from Love@ Work into your life. As Olivia writes, "we need to shine our light everywhere we go." This workbook provides exercises and lessons to lead you to a deeper look at self-love, self-mastery, self-acceptance and, most important, self-forgiveness. With gentle nudging and humor, she guides you to polish those rough edges and turn up that bright light that is you!

Jeanne Alford
Executive Coach, Media and Communications
www.alfordcommunications.com
www.beclear101.com

ENDNOTES

1 When someone says "You are this or that, it puts them in a position of authority. Using "I" messages allows you to feel more equal to the person complimenting you.

2 https://www.quora.com/Who-said-the-phrase-Holding-a-grudge-is-like-drinking-poison-and-waiting-for-the-other-person-to-die

3 Martha Beck, "Finding Your Way in a Wild New World," (NY, NY: Free Press, 2012) p xiii.

4 https://www.goodtherapy.org/learn-about-therapy/types/breathwork

5 https://www.somatictherapy.net/

6 https://www.changeworksinc.com/what-is-clear/

7 http://www.hellingerpa.com/constellation.shtml

8 Ibid p 56.

9 https://thetrustfrequency.net/

10 Brené Brown, "Dare to Lead." (London, Penguin Random House 2018) p 43.

11 https://www.thoughtco.com/what-is-nonverbal-communication-1691351

12 http://www.debonogroup.com/six_thinking_hats.php

46694183R00110

Made in the USA
Middletown, DE
31 May 2019